AMERICAN QUILTS

A Sampler of Quilts and Their Stories

Jennifer Regan

GALLERY BOOKS
An Imprint of W. H. Smith Publishers Inc.
112 Madison Avenue
New York City 10016

For my mother, who gave me the pieces, and my friend
who helps me put them together.

ACKNOWLEDGMENTS

Tom Bell, Doris Bowman, John Butz, Lois
Dater, William Ferris, Laura Fisher, Karla
Friedlich, Gene Hawes, Alan Isaksen,
Tracy Jamar, Nancy Katz, Joel & Kate
Kopp, Nancy W. Livingston, Irene Preston
Miller, Heidi Read, Julie Silber, Bernice
Steinbaum, Geralyn Torrone, David
Visser, Yvonne Wardwell, Shelly Zegart

This edition published in 1989 by Gallery Books, an
imprint of W. H Smith Publishers, Inc., 112 Madison
Avenue, New York, New York 10016.

Gallery Books are available for bulk purchase for sales
promotions and premium use. For details write or
telephone the Manager of Special Sales, W. H. Smith
Publishers, Inc., 112 Madison Avenue, New York, New
York 10016. (212) 532-6600.

Editorial development and design by Combined Books,
Inc., 26 Summit Grove Ave., Bryn Mawr, PA 19010.

Produced by Wieser & Wieser, Inc., 118 East 25th
Street, New York, NY 10010.

Printed in Spain by
Printer Industria Gráfica, S.A. Barcelona
D.L.B.: 32240-1989

CONTENTS

Noah's Ark Quilt.

The Macy Family Sampler Quilt was done in Maine during the last quarter of the 19th century. The quilt contains the first names of many family members and their roles within the family—aunts and an uncle, Momma and Poppa, Grandma and Grandpa. The quilt also includes traditional and original designs.

Macy Family Sampler Quilt.

Introduction

Every quilt has a story to tell. Each early American patchwork quilt, made from scraps of worn clothing or leftover fabric, speaks silently, but eloquently, of the virtues that built America—diligence, thrift, perseverance, patience, devotion to family. We envision women in New England or on their way west, in colonial houses, temporary shelters, log cabins, putting together piece by piece bits of cloth to warm their families. At first the quilts were unplanned, randomly assembled. Then they evolved into geometric shapes arranged in a repetitious design, soothingly predictable. The patchwork quilt has become a symbol of the American woman's life, pieced as her life is pieced, from the bits of fabric, bits of time, she could snatch from her main focus of caring for others. As a mother warms and comforts, protects from the cold, the quilt mirrors in its materials and make-up these same qualities.

As American society developed, quilt making changed. Piecing a quilt became more than a solitary woman working under hardship conditions to make something useful, something urgently needed, out of scraps. Repeated geometric shapes done in the limited colors and fabrics available in the early 19th century gave way to designs that showed off the quilter's skill and her eye for color. Shapes and colors, flowers and foliage, from the natural world bloomed on quilts. Women began gathering to show off their needlework, to finish off a quilt together. Quilts were made not just for families' use but as gifts, celebrations, documents of events in lives.

Quilts have always made personal statements. Early American women didn't have much time for journal-keeping, but they had to make quilts. A quilt could tell the story of a life, a place, an idea, sometimes as clearly, when it was placed against its historical background, as a book. A favorite type of quilt was the album quilt, named for the autograph album which, with a different signature on every page, is itself like a story book.

Quilts, the major creative object made by women during the greater part of America's past, went out of fashion during the early part of this century as the pace of life quickened, and manufactured goods became a household's staples, putting handcrafts in disfavor as the necessary activity of the poor. But with the renewed interest in crafts during the '60s, women developed a greater respect for all types of handwork. They renewed their commitment to their inheritance and creative activities with textiles. Then, in the 70s, the quilt gained status as artwork. Contemporary quilters applied fine arts training to quilting skills and methods. Quilts began to reflect artistic trends, feminist positions, personal feelings.

Over the decades stories behind quilts have ranged from mere hints, intriguing details that pique the curiosity of the viewer, to records of cultural trends, variations of familiar stories from folklore and literature. Today autobiographical statements grace art gallery walls and quilt shows. The sampler of quilts in this book—"sampler" refers to the kind of quilt made of a number of blocks, each of which represents a different quilt pattern—provides a selection of the kinds of stories women have told in their quilts. In doing so, it records American history: public memories of wars, migrations, and good works, as well as personal hopes and sorrows. Not all quilts in this sampler are beautiful. Some are included because of bizarre stories behind them rather than the eye-and-soul appeal for which quilts are beloved. *AMERICAN QUILTS* conserves only a tiny sampling of the volumes women have told and continue to tell with fabric, needles and thread.

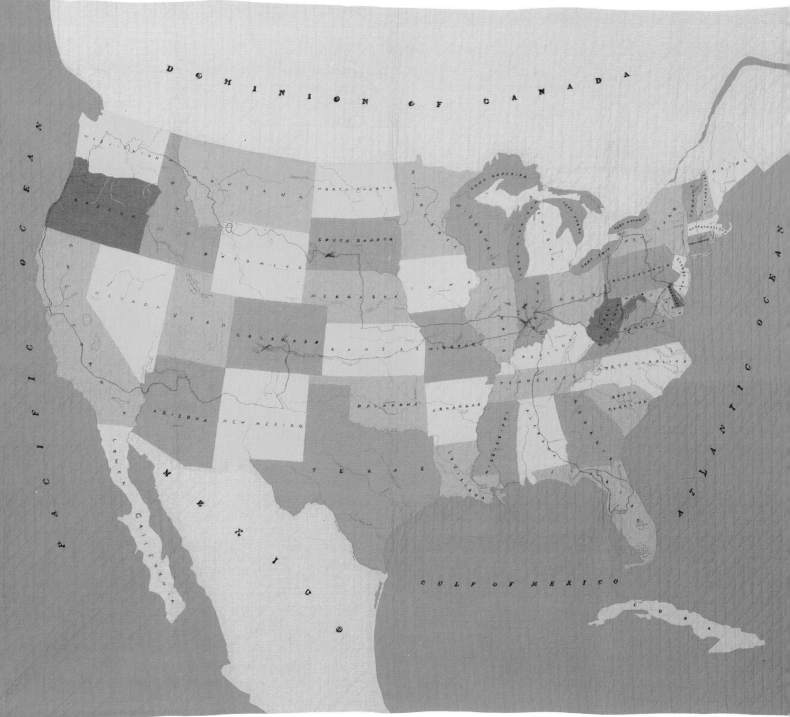

United States Map Quilt.

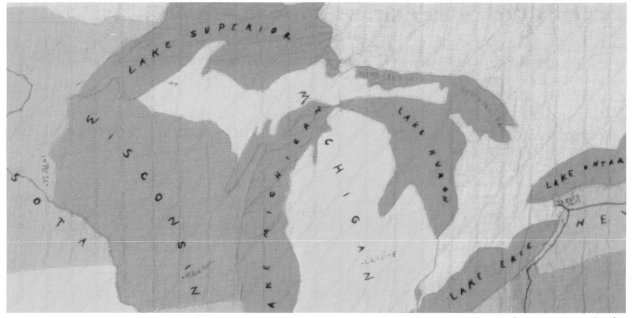

United States Map Quilt.

JOURNEYS

America is a nation of travelers, a sampler of peoples who have endured long, usually arduous journeys, and come together with a shared vision of a better life.

In 1620 the first colonists, fleeing religious oppression, arrived in Massachusetts Bay. As the eastern seaboard was settled, some undertook more journeys, pushing westward into Kentucky, Tennessee, Ohio. At the close of the Revolutionary War what had been a trickle became a torrent. Nowhere in the world has an area the size of America's West been settled in so short a time, mostly at the initiative of individuals or small groups.

The decade following the War of 1812 was known as the Great Migration. Through the Cumberland Gap, across the Shenandoah, the Ohio, the Missouri, the Mississippi, pioneers pushed westward, over the Rockies, across the desert. Between 1850 and 1860 the population of the upper Mississippi increased 167 percent, assuring the

North's victory in the Civil War. Even during the war, droves of adventurers, lured by reports of gold and silver discoveries, headed for Colorado, Oregon, California. In the '70s and '80s the Great Plains—America's last frontier—were settled.

Except for the Civil War, no event in the last century has been so thoroughly documented as the westward migration. Diaries and journals report roads crowded with covered wagons, cavalcades of well-to-do plantation owners, flatboats laden with livestock floating down rivers.

While early photographers traveled west to record the phenomenon, women stitched their thoughts and feelings into their quilts, assembling from their bags of pieces—piece bags—patterns with some kind of order as they faced the unknown. Having often been forced to uproot, leave their families and acquaintances, and follow their husbands, the women gathered at night in wagon camps, visiting with each other, trading the day's adventures, exchanging reflections on their journeys—sickness, death, bad weather, dangerous encounters, discoveries, adjustments.

Over many decades Blacks were brought by force tragically from Africa to shoulder a distortion of a dream of prosperity. Meanwhile, immigrants from Europe continued to flee economic deprivation, overcrowding, and religious oppression in search of new beginnings in America. After the 1830s, improved transportation and advertising for labor brought wave after wave of immigrants, infected by what was known as "America fever," to "dollar land."

The lure of freedom in all areas continues to draw the disenfranchised to America's shores. Like the early colonists, women bring their native needlework traditions with them, adapting them to new lives. Bred now into the native-born American seems to be a characteristic restlessness and curiosity that is surely rooted in our early wanderings. Through it all, women have kept journals of all types of journeys in their quilts.

UNITED STATES MAP QUILT

**Piecing and embroidery
Indianapolis, Indiana, 1930
Collection of Shelly Zegart's Quilts
72 inches by 88 inches**

This charming *United States Map Quilt* was made to commemorate a family's auto trip West. Starting in Indiana, it traces the family's northern and southern routes to and from California, highlighted with embroidered state names and rivers, with the names of state capitals inscribed in India ink.

The quilt is entirely pieced, with each state a separate piece of fabric. Piecing is the technique of sewing small bits of fabric together to form a larger overall sheet. The vast majority of quilts made in America since 1750 have been pieced. Piecing has always appealed to the American quilter, who saw it as a means of making something from almost nothing, constructing a usable cloth from bits and pieces too small to be useful in themselves. Piecing a quilt satisfies thrift and economy which are among the virtues at the very heart of the early American dream. In 1829 Lydia Mary Child cataloged the duties of women in realizing their families' dream in a widely regarded book *The Frugal Housewife.* In it she described the newly defined science of household economy as "the art of gathering up all fragments, so that nothing is lost."*

*p. 64, *Hearts and Hands: The Influence of Women and Quilts on American Society.* Pat Ferrero, Elaine Hedges, Julie Silber. The Quilt Digest Press. 1987.

Use of Ink

The use of ink in inscribing quilts was common practice on quilts in the 19th century. As late as 1830 families were still making their own ink, often with an iron component that rotted fabric. In 1841 an indelible writing ink was patented in France, then in the United States by Thomas J. Spear, so that inscriptions on quilts would survive rather than fade into a rotted groove.

There was always a debate as to what was best to use to write on quilts—the gray goose quill or steel-pointed pen. The writing itself on this quilt, as on others of the period, is typically elaborate. In 1848 Platt Rogers Spence published his book that launched the flowery Spencerian method of handwriting. Special classes in penmanship were taught separately from public education, and calligraphic flourishes decorated many quilts.

Piecing

Piecing the design of a quilt requires the use of templates. These are pattern pieces for each shape in a given design. They can be made of metal or wood, but heavy cardboard is just as effective. A shape is traced on and cut out from the cardboard; then as many of the shapes as the pattern requires are traced onto fabric. These shapes are cut out, adding enough extra fabric all around to use as a seam. The pieces are then seamed together with other shapes to make up the quilt's design.

Most shapes used in traditional quilt designs are geometric in nature. The most frequently used geometric shapes are the diamond, square, rectangle, triangle, rhomboid, pentagon, hexagon, octagon, and parts of circles—that is, quarter- or half-circles.

Afro-American quilters talk about "building a quilt," and indeed, putting together a geometric pattern is like building with blocks, or bricks, both of which have patterns named for them. The simplest pieced quilts are based on patterns consisting of the repetition of one shape, the Ninepatch (or Threepatch) being the most familiar. In it nine squares of similar dimensions are the basis of a variety of designs which can contain triangles or other shapes with the squares, depending on what visual effect the quilter is seeking. The main rule for piecing is that designs should be planned to allow for as much straight-seam piecing as possible. Sewing into angles and sewing curved seams is more complex than straight-seam sewing.

The United States Map is a masterful achievement in piecing. A separate template, or pattern, had to be made for each state so that the pattern was like a jigsaw puzzle of America. It must have been quite a chore to piece the curved and indented borders of states such as Kentucky and Montana, and Florida. Parallel lines of stitching hold the quilt together.

DOUBLE NINEPATCH

Piecing in wools and some rayon
Lancaster, Pennsylvania, c. 1940
Esprit Collection
Photographed by Sharon Risendorph and Lynn Kellner

Double Ninepatch is an apt name for the pattern of this quilt done mostly in brilliant blue and purple. The Ninepatch squares within the blocks are mirrored in the Ninepatch composition of the blocks themselves. Colors in the overall pattern are arranged to emphasize the quilt's center. Synthetic fabrics, such as rayon crepe used in this mostly wool quilt, were common in later Lancaster pieces.

Feather scrolling stitches fill the purple band and extend into the blue outer corner blocks in graceful curves. The inner black band is quilted with a flower within a diamond. The Ninepatch blocks are quilted in squares; in other words, placed so that they are a diamond on a square. Immense and elaborate medallions, or stylized flowers, with intricately interlocking rings fill the blue spaces with half motifs in the blue triangles around the edges. In truth, in what appears to be empty space of a square or diamond shape between the patches, the seamstress has juxstaposed an elaborate curvilinear design in the midst of a strictly geometric composition.

Double Ninepatch Quilt.

Graveyard Quilt.

Graveyard Quilt.

THE GRAVEYARD QUILT

Applique, pieced, with embroidery, c. 1839
By Elizabeth Roseberry Mitchell
Lewis County, Kentucky
The Kentucky Historical Society
81 inches by 85 inches

The Graveyard Quilt is a memory quilt, a type created to mourn a deceased person, often made from pieces of clothing and inscribed in ink or embroidery with the deceased's name, date of death and sometimes a sad verse. A quilt similar to this type was the widow's quilt, usually black and white, and for use during the period of mourning.

The seamstress, Elizabeth Roseberry Mitchell, who made this graveyard quilt was born in Pennsylvania in 1799 and moved with her family across the border into Ohio in 1830. Two sons died and were buried there before the Mitchell family left a failed farm and moved on to Kentucky. Because of the high death rate among children, and of adults

from disease, death was a constant companion of 19th century Americans. Elizabeth Mitchell was typical of her time in that she lost two sons. and she had to leave their graves behind when she and her family moved on to what they hoped were truly greener pastures. Mrs. Mitchell began the quilt after a visit back to her sons' graves. The worn condition suggests she slept under it, perhaps to be near her sons—a morbid kind of comforter, indeed, by today's standards. Elizabeth Mitchell died in an epidemic in 1856.

The *Graveyard Quilt* is a unique example of its kind. In the center is the family plot with four coffins marked with paper tags, each bearing a

13

family member's name. The large coffin in the middle also includes dates. Quilting stitches outline spaces for thirteen additional coffins. More coffins are outlined or appliqued around the border of the quilt. Mrs. Mitchell's plan was to move a coffin from the quilt's edge into the center plot as a family member died.

Around the family plot is the same brown fence that borders the quilt's outside edge. Delicate trees with pink rosebuds and green leaves are embroidered over the gate and along the fence. Pink-flowered vines border the pathway that leads to the center square. The elaborate gate may well have had a name at the top on the applique that is totally worn off now so that only the outline remains. The blossoms and vines are more detailed and profuse at the entrance to the plot. Blooms are white and yellow as well as rose. Leaf shapes show variety and some are quite feathery. The heavy fenceposts at the corners are surrounded with blooms in yellow and cream.

Of the eleven additional coffins in the upper margin, all have names except for one. Five appear as a possible family at the top center; three are small, two larger. In the bottom margin of the quilt there are nine coffins with names. It appears that other coffins once appliqued in this area have been removed. The actual quilting between the outside fence and the calico blocks that forms the basis of the quilt is done in coffin outlines.

Graveyard Quilt.

Brown calico* squares alternate with squares of the LeMoyne or Lemon Star pattern done in browns, tan, cream, reds and rose. The eight-pointed star of this pattern is composed from diamond shapes. As long as American women have made quilts, the star and its many variations have been popular. The LeMoyne is one of the earliest star patterns and is the foundation for many other star patterns, as well as tulip and lily designs.

LeMoyne was the name of two brothers who founded New Orleans in 1718. The story goes that they became unpopular after they claimed more and more land from France, so up North this pattern was called Lemon. However, "Lemon" may be a bastardization of the name "LeMoyne."

*p. 104, *Quilts in America*. Patsy and Myron Orlofsky. McGraw-Hill, 1974. Calico "refers to cottons with printed small-scale, sometimes minute, conventionalized patterns often in not over two colors" and has been the "granddaddy and mainstay of all quilt fabrics." The name derives from cotton imported by the East India Company of Calicut.

Quilt Names

The names of a quilt pattern very often depended on the locales where the quilt was made and is a significant clue for dating and placing a quilt in a locale. Until the 19th century names were passed orally from one generation to another. The hundreds of quilt names reflect the diversity of the imaginations that shaped America.

In *Quilts in America*** authors Patsy and Myron Orlofsky report that a collector of quilts names had counted 4000 by 1974 when their book came out. Names have changed over the years, they tell us, citing as an example the Job's Tears pattern that was named at first for the decorative seed growing on the garden plant. When slavery became a burning issue, the name changed to Slave Chain. In 1840, with Northern sentiment against the

annexation of Texas, another slave state, it was called Texas Tears. After the Civil War it became the Rocky Road to Kansas and finally ended up as Endless Chain, perhaps in reference to the expansion and industrialization of the country which had formed a "chain" of development from coast to coast. In addition to differences over the decades, pattern names changed to fit situations and local history. Beth Gutcheon, author of *The Perfect Patchwork Primeer*,*** points out that Duck Foot in the Mud, on Long Island, is known as Hand of Friendship in Quaker Philadelphia and Bear's Paw in Ohio.

**Ibid., p. 245.

***p. 32, *The Perfect Patchwork Primer*.

Early quilt names honored revolutionary heroes like Washington's Quilt, Martha Washington's Star. Historic events have always provided quilt names. There was a Segregation quilt, a Union quilt. The Lincoln's Platform quilt is said to have been designed during the Lincoln-Douglas debates, proving that although women did not at the time have suffrage, they were well-informed on politics.

Pattern names rooted in religion mirrored the deep faith of American settlers who brought some pattern names to America from their countries of origin. Garden of Eden was a pattern name that signified the expectations of immigrants and pioneers; Jacob's Ladder and World Without End were other biblical names. Names came from trades—Carpenter's Wheel; activities, such as the square dances often held in conjunction with quilting bees—Hands All Around. Names were personalized with names of public figures—Martha Washington's Star; and private ones—Mary's Rising Sun was made by quilter Mary Totten of Staten Island, who was born in 1781. Her heirs passed along her name with her quilt. Names could also teach moral lessons: Drunkard's Path, also called Fool's Puzzle

and Country Husband, is a pattern that winds—one could say staggers—all over the quilt.

Of course, nature was an obvious and rich source for quilt pattern names; there are countless patterns named for trees and flowers from all over the country—Prairie Flower, Tulips, Pine Tree, plus all types of names based on roses. Historically a flower of symbolism and high esteem, the rose was the flower name used most often. The type of rose, Moss or California, can often be used to date a quilt.

From the 1830s on, named quilt patterns were reproduced in magazines such as *Godey's Lady's Book* in the same way they are today in *Ladies' Home Journal*.

What's in a name? might well be a logical question for anyone studying quilt patterns and their often fantastic and whimsical names. But, except for one-of-a-kind quilts that have been passed down in families, like the Graveyard Quilt, quilt names are lost in history along with the identities of the mostly anonymous women who made them.

EVENING STAR

Piecing of cottons, c. 1925
Midwest Amish
Courtesy Esprit Collection
Photographed by Sharon Risedorph and Lynn Kellner

The Evening Star crib quilt is a nine-star pattern set within a combination of narrow and wide borders typical of Midwestern Amish quilts. The colors selected and the manner in which they are combined demonstrate an artistic sensitivity in the construction of a utilitarian object. The striking contrasts between lights and darks would catch a baby's eye even though familiar objects are not portrayed here.

Two deep blue stars and two of rose fabric alternate with pale pink stars around the center star. Triangles and squares were pieced with others in black before the individual quilt blocks were joined. Great care was taken and needlework was very precise to assure that the tips of the points come together and just barely touch.

The nine blocks are contained within a border of pale blue inside a wide black band edged in the rose fabric. The color of the quilting thread changes with the color of the fabric to make the

quilting as inconspicuous as possible. The wide side black borders are quilted in groups of three diagonal lines. The top and bottom black band have a stylized tulip shape at the center and a pair of large leaves with decorative veins and intertwining vines on each side that fill the space. A simple chain with interspersed diamonds quilts the pale turquoise band.

Evening Star Quilt.

Hmong Story Cloth.

Hmong Story Cloth.

HMONG STORY CLOTH

Piecing and embroidery, 1987
By Chiang Xiong, Laotian born
United States
Wadsworth Atheneum, Florence Paull Berger Fund
55 inches by 57 inches

The Hmong Story Cloth depicts Chiang Xiong's flight from Laos. "Hmong" means literally "free people." The Hmong, or Miao, as they are known in China, where they number more than five million, are a nomadic people who today live in the hills of continental Southeast Asia and, in increasing numbers, the United States. Thousands of Hmong recruits from Laos fought beside American soldiers during the war in Vietnam. When Laos fell to North Vietnam in the '70s, families were forced to flee. The United States set up refugee camps in Thailand. There the women began to create story cloths that record both their traditional textile traditions and their struggle for freedom.

Chiang Xiong now lives with her family in Providence, Rhode Island, the New England population center for her people. She and her family have become American citizens, like many other Hmong, whose skills have proved valuable in the clothing industry in the United States. In Lancaster County, Pennsylvania, where about sixty Hmong families have settled near the Amish communities, quilts are big tourist business. Instead of producing their native story cloths, virtually all the Hmong women resettled there sew quilts that are sold in local tourist stores and advertised as "locally made." Quilt making there is so lucrative that many Hmong women have abandoned their traditional embroidery altogether while some continue

Chiang Xiong.

to embroider only costumes for themselves and their children to wear on holidays.

Just as in colonial America girls were taught to sew and to make quilts at a very young age, young Hmong girls learned the art of "pa ndau," a sophisticated way of sewing without pins or patterns that produces twenty stitches to an inch. It appears, because of the uniformity and neatness of the work, to have been accomplished by machine. (In Western quilts, ten stitches per inch is regarded as fine work through the three layers of fabric.)

This story cloth is a typical one made by refugees. In the upper right corner is the village where Chiang Xiong and her neighbors lived. A white plane swoops down over the village and men in green uniforms fire rifles at the fleeing villagers. Pigs, chickens, a water buffalo and goats escape from the noisy guns. Several groups of villagers head straight for the river. As they file through the jungle they pass beautiful flowering trees where monkeys play (right center), flowers bloom, and butterflies cavort in the treetops. Exotic birds watch the fleeing villagers from their perches in the trees (upper left center).

Documenting the most terrifying events of the long journey to the refugee camp, Chiang Xiong includes the ordeal of crossing the Mekong River which separates Laos from Thailand. Chiang is represented throughout by the woman carrying a baby on her back. A woman swimming across the river between the green log raft at right and the yellow boat has a baby on her back. There is another raft further up river as well as some commercial boat traffic. Note that in the area of the river where the woman with the baby swims, one person is trying to get across on a log while another has a log under each arm for support.

In the upper left where the river disappears into the mountains is a refugee encampment. It seems that some groups at first left their village to hide in the mountains, but probably the hovering military helicopter chased them out. They have temporary shelters set up. One man seems to be planting a tree, while another picks something from a tree. A woman cooks over a fire while another does chores in the shelter. Their baskets and burdens are strewn about. Note the white teakettle in the hands of the woman at the front of those arriving. Two of the women in the right corner are carrying similar white objects, which is proof of the importance of this piece of household goods.

After the refugees have succeeded in crossing the river they are greeted by a different breed of military man at the large refugee camp reception center. He appears rather brusque as he directs the people to the waiting trucks. The military man by the orange truck also carries a rifle, but it is slung over his shoulder and he holds the end of the barrel. The two soldiers by the trucks, keeping an eye on the scene, but not working too hard, are decorated as officers. Those directing the refugees have the appearance of privates—no decorations, khakis blouse over their boots and the sleeves are rolled up—a reminder of the hot climate. After the truck ride side in the lower left, the woman sits while the man tries to manage the paperwork. Note that the woman with the baby has already arrived and awaits the others.

Several details of the story cloth are interesting. See the various configurations of the buildings. Behind the welcoming privates are gray permanent office buildings, of much smaller perspective than the refugee huts set up off the ground on stilts. The smaller two-sided huts certainly look like wash houses and latrines. Back along the highway with blue cars on the way to the airport are larger thatched roof buildings, apparently for some group use, which are also set up on stilts.

Many of the fine details of the scene are embroidered. The depiction of the vegetation is especially noteworthy. The bamboo growing along the river has graceful boughs as do the palm fronds along the highway at the end of the refugee encampment. The tree at lower right center with the monkey and butterflies is a lovely composition in itself. It is reminiscent of what might be seen on a colonial American quilt. The leaves and flowers are carefully delineated and bright green parrots occupy the tree with the monkey and another light-colored beast. It is like a Garden of Eden, and that is probably the way Chiang Xiong remembers her homeland.

The decorative border in white and blue completes the composition. There are two bands of blue and two of white with the sawtoothed edge of pieced blue triangles between. Strictly speaking, this quilt, made for display rather than use as bedding, is not the three-layer textile sandwich we know by that term. It was included in the show Drunken Paths and Ladders to the Stars at the Wadsworth Atheneum in Hartford, however, because of its use of piecing, embroidery and other techniques used in quilt making, even though it lacks the middle interlining of a quilt.

Quilt Construction

In three-layer quilts the interlining was traditionally made of one of several materials, chosen for warmth, softness and ease of sewing. Before the invention of the cotton gin by Eli Whitney in 1793, quilts were stuffed with the less desirable clippings from sheep, or with cotton grown in South Carolina or Georgia (where slaves took the cotton from the boll and removed the seeds in a grueling time-consuming process), or exported by England from her colonies in the West Indies. Also used for linings were flannels, and worn-out old quilts. For bedding which was not quilted, cornhusks, goose feathers, even dried leaves or paper were used to add bulk and warmth.

With the invention of the cotton gin, a mechanism which mimicked the slave woman's clawing at the cotton boll with her fingernails, cotton began to be the most common substance used for linings. As early as the mid-19th century cotton was available as batting in sheets large enough to line a quilt. Today's quilters can choose between cotton and dacron battings. Many now prefer dacron as it doesn't demand the close quilting cotton-lined quilts demand to prevent shifting and bunching.

Hmong Story Cloth.

Adam and Eve Quilt.

Adam and Eve Quilt.

GARDENS OF EDEN

If journeys are an inevitable feature of the American experience, coming home, or creating a home, is the ultimate goal of such journeys. As the difficulties of a journey's beginnings—oppression, poverty, even sickness and war—receded into the past, and industrialization drew people together into communities of mutual help, life in the home became less difficult for the 19th century homemaker, especially with the many new conveniences.

The sewing machine, patented in 1846 by Elias Howe, Jr., lightened women's workload. Mass marketing by Howe and Isaac Singer started in 1856, and by 1860 over 130,000 home sewing machines had been sold. In the year 1876 alone, Singer Sewing Machine, only one of the companies marketing machines, sold more than 260 thousand. By the 1870s bedcoverings could be mail ordered from Montgomery Ward and E.C. Allen, eliminating some of the sewing necessary to keep a home running well and warmly. Women were free to do more leisurely and inventive quilt making.

Meanwhile, a textile revolution had taken place, with imports and American-manufactured fabrics using new dyes that produced bold new colors. Although severe geometric shapes and somber colors were still the choice of many quilters in the second half of the 19th century, others were interested in creating fanciful and personalized quilts.

That is not to say that simpler quilts, put together for primarily utilitarian use, did not continue to be made. Pioneers were still making the journey west and new settlers lived under Spartan or worse conditions where design was secondary to usefulness, and haste before the winter season set in was required. But even Western settlers felt the shift towards a more leisurely domestic life so that beauty often merged with necessity. Even women traveling west were urged to let the men conquer the wilderness while they settled their homes, making of them "domestic Edens."* Scraps of bright material were assembled into quilt patterns containing flowers and vines. Often a woman had two quilts going at once, one of a simple geometric pattern she could work on absent mindedly and in bad light, the other, frequently an applique quilt, she could create at leisure, emphasizing decorative qualities and fine workmanship as important considerations.

Eden was as appropriate a metaphor for the wilderness the settlers set out to tame, as it had been for those who earlier arrived on America's shores. The Garden of Eden was, in fact, used in late 19th century promotional literature as a symbol of America: a pamphlet with which an employer hoped to lure cheap labor from Scandinavia pictured gold bricks and plenty of women and described America as a Garden of Eden.

At a time when religious faith was a major source of strength, the church was a center of social and spiritual life. With the Bible a major source of storytelling and symbolism, it is not surprising that

the Garden of Eden was a popular symbol for the home as a refuge from the outside world, a place where, with typical American optimism and enthusiasm, women would try to recreate the idealism inherent in man's, and woman's, very first "home."

The gentler life style of 19th century America is reflected in the pains taken in quilted versions of the Garden of Eden. It was often the design chosen for a bride's quilt, one presented to a bride and saved for best, thus preserving it so that many such quilts survive today. Vines and flowers, birds and other animals, decorate the individual quilter's presentations of the story which inevitably feature Adam and Eve and the snake, as well as the Tree of Life. In each version, social customs and individual skills of the quilter are revealed, as well as her unique appreciation of the story at the base of Christian and Judaic civilization.

Adam and Eve Quilt.

ADAM AND EVE QUILT

Applique
Probably Pennsylvania, c. 1850
Abby Aldrich Rockefeller Folk Art Center
Williamsburg, Virginia

This colorful *Adam and Eve Quilt* consists of nine blocks appliqued with stylized trees and flowers, birds and animals, and a red calico Adam and Eve. Like the greatest number of American quilts, it is composed of sections called blocks which are sewn together to make up the quilt's top.

Applique quilts, though sometimes thought to have developed as a type later than pieced quilts, were made concurrently. Contrary to another popular assumption, although they could be as

humble as pieced quilts and were often regarded as purely everyday, they could be extremely complex and elegant. Also, the word "patchwork," generally thought to be synonymous with "pieced," actually describes applique quilts as well; both types are made of patches, either seamed together as in pieced quilts, or applied to a background, or ground fabric. Applique, also called laid-on work, comes from the French word meaning "applied."

Adam and Eve Quilt.

The applique quilt, considered in the 19th century as the aristocrat of quilts, reached its peak of excellence in the Baltimore area in the middle of the century. Often designed to spotlight the quilter's eye for design and color, the applique quilt frequently drew upon nature for its material, using foliage and flowers to great effect. Whereas pieced quilts were usually geometric in design, applique quilts were likely to be pictorial. They can be divided into two groups: symmetrical designs, and freely drawn designs, in which anything that can be drawn with pen, paintbrush and paints is replicated with fabric and the quilter's needle and thread.

Templates were made for use in cutting applique pieces, as they were for geometric designs. For symmetrical applique designs, a pattern is cut from folded paper in the same way a child makes a snowflake from a paper pattern, and used over and over. For freeform designs, each shape requires a separate template.

This Adam and Eve quilt combines a symmetrical pattern in the Rose of Sharon design with the artist's free form adaptation of the Adam and Eve story. The stylized, naive interpretations of flowers and other subjects make the quilt an example of folk art. Probably from Pennsylvania, it has features typical of that area where bright colors and highly stylized forms interpret traditional quilt patterns from the vantage point of persons working without inhibitions to turn nature into art.

The variations in color, mostly reds and yellows, and shapes, in which no attempt has been made to achieve precision of measurement, give the quilt a carefree, lyrical quality. This Adam and Eve, arms raised, could be marveling at the beauty of Paradise, a fitting pose for what was no doubt a bridal quilt.

Traditionally, rose names appeared in the most popular floral patterns, no doubt due to the high esteem for the flower in the general imagination. Some pattern names were Wreaths of Roses, Texas Yellow Rose, Missouri Rose and Tea Rose. Rose of Sharon, a design composed of roses, rosebuds, stems and leaves, was the most popular rose pattern and an apt choice for the Bible quilt because of its derivation from the Song of Solomon:

I am the rose of Sharon, and the lily of the valley.
As the lily among thorns, so is my love among daughters.
As the apple tree among the trees of the world, so is my beloved among the sons.

A quilt of the Rose of Sharon pattern is usually among the quilts in a young woman's dowry chest, very often the bridal quilt itself.

Adam and Eve in the Garden of Eden Quilt.

Adam and Eve in the Garden of Eden Quilt

ADAM AND EVE IN THE GARDEN OF EDEN

**Piecing and applique, cotton with some silk
last quarter of 19th century
Purchased at Arkansas church fair around 1900
Smithsonian Institution
84 inches by 74 inches**

The quilter of *Adam and Eve in the Garden of Eden* has placed vignettes from Adam and Eve's story in relation to the universe, with the sun, stars and four phases of the moon in the quilt's center. A flowering vine, a favorite design, grows from the trunk at the bottom edge of the quilt, which is scalloped. Eve is shown picking the apple, with a mean-looking snake and a butterfly watching, handing the apple to a dark-skinned Adam, and fleeing from the garden with him. Birds and butter-

flies, as well as the undulating vine, give the quilt a lyrical quality. It's interesting that, while Adam is naked, Eve is attired in a dress and apron of the time period. Perhaps the quilter's Victorian modesty prevails here.

The encircling vine has bunches of berries growing off side shoots. While white moths flutter between the scrolls of the vine and the edge of the quilt, others realistically rendered in color flit around with imaginary birds of the same size. In

25

the basically symmetrical four corners are appliques of four stylized flowering plants, almost but not quite, identical in color and fabric. Several trees bearing a variety of fruits and flowers are arranged on the sides.

At the bottom of the quilt above the base of the vine is obviously the apple tree. The huge serpent lies beneath the tree contrary to tradition, as Eve, dressed in colonial style, picks the largest fruit from the lowest branch. Her rather elaborate costume includes a bustle, petticoats, and bonnet.

Moving to the right, between the two trees, Adam takes the apple from Eve. He is not as elaborate as the Eve figure, and as previously noted, appears to be naked. Although the figure now shows considerable wear, the remnants of applique are black and white plaid and have no decorative detail. Again, note the immense size of the apple, and the ruffle on the bottom of Eve's skirt. The overskirt even has detailing around the scalloped lower edge.

At the top of the quilt, Adam flees from the garden toward a break in the vines with Eve following him. They appear to challenge gravity as they stand on a different plane from the one on which the trees grow.

The entire expanse of the firmament is represented in the scallop-edged circle in the center. The four phases of the moon, the sun, and stars are included. The beautiful sunburst in shades of rose, rust and brown is truly the center of the universe represented in this quilt. After an initial examination of the wonders of the heavens, the eye is attracted to the curling stem of the vine as it wanders from scene to scene in the Garden of Eden. The soft shades of teal, rose, tan, gold, rust, and brown predominate and are a marked contrast to the stark white of the background.

The pattern of the quilting is in overall parallel diagonal lines three-eighths inch apart. The sun, moon and larger flowers are quilted in outline, or echo quilting—that is, the stitching follows the shape of the design element.

Adam and Eve in the Garden of Eden Quilt.

Stuffing

In *Adam and Eve in the Garden of Eden*, some of the fruits are stuffed to make them stand out in relief and appear more realistic. This technique was popular during the 19th century. After the quilting was done, tiny tufts of cotton were inserted through holes pricked in the quilt's backing behind the areas to be stuffed. These had to be invisible, as the appearance of the back of a quilt was as important on fine quilts as was the front. Because of the precision required in stuffing, it is considered the ultimate in needlework skills.

Many white masterwork quilts were done using this technique, also called trapunto. According to *New Discoveries in American Quilts* [*] "the threads on the coarse backing of the quilt were carefully separated and cotton or batting was pushed through the holes. When the desired fullness had been achieved, the threads were pulled together again. After washing, the strained threads generally shrank together tightly, thus firmly securing the stuffing inside."

[*]p. 99, *New Discoveries in American Quilts*. F.P. Dutton, 1975.

Adam and Eve in the Garden of Eden Quilt.

The Quilting Process

Quilting is the process by which the three layers of a quilt are sewn together with a running stitch so that the inner layer of batting won't shift. Quilts can also be fastened by tying, a technique in which a stitch is made, the ends drawn up through the design side of the quilt, cut and tied. Tying was used in everyday quilts, or in the later crazy quilts when materials used were too heavy to quilt, and patterns were random and often decorated with stitchery.

There are two kinds of quilting patterns: filler as that used in the Smithsonian Garden of Eden quilt, and decorative, as in the intricate quilting on Amish quilts. Filler patterns were marked on the quilt with a ruler; templates were used for decorative designs. These were made from wood or cardboard, as they were for piercing, or paper. Marking a quilt for quilting was considered an art in the 19th century; not everyone could do it, and often professional needlewomen were hired to mark quilts. For the confident marker, designs could be drawn on freehand.

There are many techniques for marking a quilt. The "pricking and pouncing" technique (described by the Orlovskys) involves laying a paper pattern template on the area to be quilted and pricking holes through it with a pencil along the pattern's outline. Holes can be made in the template with a sharp instrument and the paper dusted—fireplace ash, cinnamon and corn starch were used—to leave easily removed markings. Light markings were important, not just marking that would wash out, as fine quilts weren't intended to be washed.

The quilting itself was regarded as the highest art employed in quilt making in the 18th and 19th centuries. Its quality was judged on stitches being as small and as evenly spaced as possible. Some quilting is so perfect that it appears to have been done by machine. It should not be possible to see where thread begins and ends. Large, clumsy stitches were called "toenail-catchers."

Like quilt patterns themselves, quilting designs had names which, as in the former, often depended on the locales where quilts were made. Filler designs had such names as diagonal (the design used in this quilt), diamond, herringbone, and so forth. Among decorative designs used were feather wreath, fan, cross and rosettes.

Garden of Eden Quilt.

John Gordon

Garden of Eden Quilt.

GARDEN OF EDEN QUILT

Applique
By Abby F. Bell Ross
Irvington, New Jersey, 1874
Courtesy of Mr. and Mrs. Ben Mildwoff
87 inches square

A veritable paradise of brilliantly conceived birds, wild and domestic beasts, flowers and foliage, including palm trees, insects and creatures of the deep, in this *Garden of Eden* provides the stage where Adam has begun his fatal approach to a very seductive Eve. It goes without saying that the art of applique was fluorishing during the part of the 19th century when this quilt was made. The creator of this garden exhibits a knowledge of the world and access to education. Perhaps Abby Bell Ross had an acquaintance with the work of John James Audubon, popular North American naturalist. She was thoroughly aware of the birds common on the East Coast, as well as some of the exotic species.

She also found pleasure in creating some very elaborate species based on her imagination. Those shapes in the upper fourth of the quilt that appear to be stylized birds are associated with stars and are probably representations of clouds. Note the moon in the middle of a cluster of clouds and stars at the center top of the quilt.

The tree as a center motif was a very popular one. It probably originated in painted and dyed quilts imported in the 17th century from India to England. These quilts had a center featuring a large floral design. In the late 19th century imported quilts were replaced by palampores, one-piece bed covers with no interlining or backing. The central

29

design was apt to be a flowering tree. Often, the tree was cut from the palampore and appliqued as the center of a quilt. The tree, of course, had many meanings, both as the Tree of Life and for its part in the Crucifixion. And some quilters used it simply as a convenient perch for exotic birds to show off their imagination and technique.

The composition of this Garden of Eden is balanced and symmetrical. The large, but delicate, Tree of Knowledge dominates the center and the whole composition is enclosed with a gracefully looping and carefully placed vine. From the vine bloom an immense variety of flowers—most imaginary, but many based on flowers that Abby Bell Ross had herself admired in gardens or meadows, or studied in books of naturalists. The flowers are appliqued with embroidered details. Foliage in shades of white and cream fills in between the blossoms, and a trumpet-shaped flower on the left balances a similar flower on the right, and so on.

The space behind the central tree is filled with a glade of eight identical palm trees growing from blue mounds. There is variety in the curves of the tree trunks, however. (Abby Bell seemed to realize that identically straight trees would have made a static composition.) An oak and a pear spread their branches beneath the Tree of Knowledge, and there are two additional fairly complex trees, or plants, outside the vine on the line that marks the low horizon.

The configuration of the horizon line and the placement of the central tree draw the eye to Adam and Eve in the low center of the composition, but there is no real sense of perspective and above all a total disregard for size relationships in the real world.

Flitting throughout this paradise is a variety of hummingbirds, dragonflies, and butterflies which occupy considerably more space, and are far more interesting, than the two figures of Adam and Eve. All the flying creatures are matched one for similar one, side for side. Monkeys, crabs, scorpions, spiders, grasshoppers, flamingoes, ducks and other water birds scamper up and down on the blue mounds under the palms.

Moving to the center of the composition, there appears to be a male and female of many of the bird species represented. At the very top, above the vine, is a pair of eagles. In the tree, itself, are birds that appear to be owls, blue jays, a peacock, red-winged black bird, mocking bird, goldfinch, toucan, dove, cardinal, robin, and hawk. At the base of the tree, Eve reclines under an embroidered garland held in the beak of a large eagle-like bird. A skinny serpent hangs from the tree, as Eve, unashamed, dangles the apple and relaxes on a flowery mound. An eager Adam proceeds directly towards her. This is the scene that should capture the viewer, but the plethora of detail elsewhere distracts the eye.

Below the couple, romping about without regard to size or geographical origin, is a menagerie of birds and animals: a guinea hen the size of the elephant, a domestic cat, long-horned sheep, elk, bears, a tapir, giraffees, mice, shrews, squirrels, rabbits, a zebra, anteater, leopards, a lion, horse, burro, various cows and a pair of camels —all these among embroidered flowers and grasses. In two special niches beneath the vine are creatures of the sea: fish, a frog, and turtles mingled in seaweed. Balancing this is a pair of ducks with their brood waddling among grasses.

This has all been joined together in a marvelous creation by a lady with considerable leisure, skills of a fine seamstress, and knowledge of the world.

Garden of Eden Quilt.

Garden of Marriage Quilt.

THE GARDEN OF MARRIAGE

Applique and embroidery
By Jennifer Regan
New York, 1980
18 inches square, tabletop cover

The *Garden of Marriage* is a contemporary whimsical creation by the author of this book, made as a twenty-first wedding anniversary present for her husband. Designed to cover a small table in his study, it is a free-wheeling adaptation of the Abby Bell Ross Garden of Eden quilt. As the Garden of Eden was a perfect metaphor for life as it evolved in late 19th century America, so it is appropriate for one's ideas of marriage when romance and optimism dictate expectations.

The creatures in the tree are made from scraps of fabrics left over from various sewing projects. They were randomly chosen—not just birds, as in Mrs. Ross's tree—but an alligator, flying fish, grasshopper, and cats. The baby stands for the three children in the family and was appliqued from a silk summer dress, as were the Adam and Eve.

The embroidered quotations and sayings reflect attitudes about life. The "marry month of May" derives from the wedding month. The bird at top left is saying, "Nevermore," like Poe's raven, while another on the right croons, "All my pretty ones," words of Lady MacBeth after she killed her children. The brown owl at the top doesn't hoot like the conventional owl, but instead moans, "Rue, rue, rue," acknowledging the many regrets a long marriage accumulates. The enigmatic cat, made from a husband's shirt perches on a branch under the word "Howl," calling to mind the feeling of alienation of modern man and Allen Ginsberg's groundbreaking collection of poems.

The biblical line, "My roarings are poured out like water," follow the outline of Eve. Adam, on the other hand, representing a man who was always cheerful and delighted with life, has "Heart's desire, heart's delight" written at his back.

In this example the whole world is in the tree. The tree is the whole Garden of Eden. In spite of the thoughtful and somewhat anguished sentiments expressed in the embroidery, the tree is a delightful and imaginative creation. The healthy baby exhibits no fear, perched atop the hefty serpent, as she helps herself to some of the assorted fruit the tree produces. The shining sun, the batik bird, the seersucker cat, and the colorful rainbow embroidered between two upper branches make this a very personal celebration of a particular family and its memories.

The tabletop cover is finished with outline quilting around the figures and shapes in the design and completed with all-over quilting. The author did this at a very difficult time in her life. Working on this, she experienced the healing powers of quilting, the undefinable effect that is part of the emotional appeal of quilting for many women. Putting together the pieces is a comfort when life seems to be pulling apart around you. The quilting, itself, the fixing of layers firmly to each other, symbolizes the grounding of one's self, a stability.

And then the repetitive motions of the quilting—pushing the needle in and out, back and forth—produce a soothing rhythm, achieving a kind of peace, even in the eye of a storm or family crisis. The quilter today knows how the pioneer women felt, working away at their quilts as the wilderness with its unknown hardships, and daily life with its too familiar ones, threaten. Quilting helped them "carry on" just as it helps us today.

Noah's Ark Quilt.

Noah's Ark Quilt.

NOAH'S ARK with Garden of Eden

Applique and embroidery
Ohio, 1885–95
America Hurrah Antiques, NYC
76 inches by 71 inches

The creator of *Noah's Ark*, an astounding feat of biblical interpretation, has reproduced, with no inhibiting regard to perspective, a panorama of familiar Bible stories using Noah's ark for a center-piece. It is a demonstration of her fascination with animals and skill at reproducing them in applique and embroidery. Animals stream towards the ark in pairs, as well as gathering in groves of trees and inhabiting the scalloped edge of the quilt. They are so neatly shaped that the patterns for them may well have been cookie cutters, a common practice.

The appliques on the pale blue background are all done in plush velvet or velveteen in blue, black, brown, tan, red, and a mossy green for the trees. Gold embroidery floss is used to secure all the

applique as well as to provide design details. The carefully cut scalloped border is dark blue on the longer sides and black at the top and bottom of the quilt. The vignettes represented are based on history and local legend as well as the Bible. Although the construction is basically symmetrical, it is not balanced and the orientation to the outer edges is not consistent. The quilt has to be rotated and studied with considerable concentration to appreciate the intentions of the seamstress who made it.

The enclosed Garden of Eden dominates the upper right corner. It is not surprising that the artist chose to emphasize the abundance of fruit on the heavily-laden trees in the garden—fecundity seems to be her trademark. The fruit, which in-

cludes bunches of purple grapes, berries and other fruits besides the apples, is embroidered on appliqued trees. Adam and Eve are, like many of the quilt's inhabitants, dark-skinned. The snake is rather inconspicuous, as Eve hands Adam a golden yellow apple. Adam and Eve are off center, while the serpent occupies the central position under the tree, which is not significantly different in appearance from those in the rest of the garden. Watching over the scene in the upper corners of the enclosure are two angels, each holding what appears to be a palm-like frond.

Moving clockwise around the edge of the quilt are numerous depictions, many easily identified. Regardless of the historical setting, all the structures are of 19th century style and all of the towns have towering church steeples. Directly left of the garden surrounded by trees, the sacrificial pile of logs burns as Abraham contemplates the bound Issac with the lamb in the foreground. Fire streams down on the burning city of Sodom, beyond which velvet angels climb an embroidered ladder above the sleeping Jacob. At the base of the quilt is a complete scene of men arriving on horseback at the outskirts of a city. Above that in the center near the animals entering the ark is Moses and the Burning Bush. Near the grove of trees in the lefthand corner is David standing over the slain Goliath and Daniel winning a battle with the lion. Around the corner, Moses holds up the tablets with the Ten Commandments above a tall brown velvet church steeple. Armies march in formation in the presence of soldiers on horseback carrying lances. Another city is consumed by fire and dead

Noah's Ark Quilt.

men hang from trees (note the detail of the branches). Behind a pair of pink flamingoes at the center top of the quilt, Joseph leads Mary on the donkey and three red bodies are crucified on three crosses in front of a crowd of people. Finally, back at the side of the Garden of Eden, the Good Samaritan leaves his horse to rescue the man at the side of the road.

The ark in the center dominates the composition. Among the pairs of animals entering the structure are leopards, camels, zebras, flamingoes, elk, rabbits, lions, raccoons, squirrels, elephants, rhinoceros, bears and hippopotamusus. The many stories illustrated from the Old and the New Testament make this quilt of interest to both Jewish and Christian scholars.

Noah's Ark Quilt.

The Beautiful and Unequaled Gardens of Eden and Elenale Quilt.

The Beautiful and Unequaled Gardens of Eden and Elenale Quilt.

THE BEAUTIFUL AND UNEQUALED GARDENS OF EDEN AND ELENALE

Applique
Hawaiian Islands, pre-1918
Attributed to a male quilter
Honolulu Academy of the Arts
86 inches by 98 inches

The *Beautiful and Unequaled Gardens of Eden and Elenale* is from Hawaii. With its lush vegetation and beneficient climate, Hawaii is probably as close to paradise as any earthly spot could be, making the Garden of Eden a natural subject choice for the quilter. This quilt named "Na Kihapai Nani Lua Ole O Edena" pictures both the garden of Eden and a garden from popular fiction. The inscription on the quilt's left side translates, "The embrace of a commandment." Elenale, above whose head a crown is suspended, appears to be the one in command. On the other side, in the Garden of

The Beautiful and Unequaled Gardens of Eden and Elenale Quilt.

Eden, Adam and Eve are covering themselves, suggesting they have already eaten the apple and feel shame.

Elenale was an otherworldly hero raised in a magical garden. The tale of his romance with an earthly princess, serialized in a magazine in the early 1900s, was the first known literature to be written and published in the Hawaiian language. Elenale's sizable princess closely resembles Queen Emma, a member of the royal household before Hawaii became a United States territory in 1900. Physical amplitude was an essential characteristic of Hawaiian beauty and status, required of Hawaiian royalty as a prerequisite to retaining the awe and respect of their subjects. In his book *Hawaii*, James Michener describes members of the royal family being forcefed to keep them "in shape."

Quilting was introduced to the Hawaiian Islands by missionaries from the United States who arrived there around 1820. At that time, native Hawaiians were making their clothing, bed coverings and burial wrappings from tapa, a paperlike fabric made from bark. Women used wooden mallets to pound the bark thin, then decorated it. Bed coverings were called "Kapa moe." After Captain Cook and his crew discovered the islands in 1778, Hawaiians began to copy the patterns they saw in European fabrics in pen and ink hand-drawn decorations on the tapa.

The Hawaiians were eager to imitate the ways of what they considered a superior culture, and it was in the Hawaiian nature to adapt to change. Missionaries disapproved of the natives' immodest attire and encouraged the wearing of the loose-fitting muu muu, probably copied from New England nightgowns. Missionary wives at first taught members of the royal household to make patchwork quilts; eventually quilt making was taught in the missionary schools. Frequently the muu muu was quilted after the skill was acquired.

Hawaiian natives considered it foolish to cut new fabrics into little bits and sew them back together again into a patchwork quilt. Since the muu muu was cut from full widths of fabric, they had no scrap bags in their households. Therefore, the applique quilt had greater appeal than the patchwork quilt. In addition, the greater prestige of the applique quilts no doubt caused Hawaiians to emulate them. Thus the unique Hawaiian quilt style came into being as a specific type, known as the *Kapa.*

The chief feature of the Hawaiian quilt is large, single fabric applique designs cut in one piece and sewn to a background fabric which is usually white. Paper patterns folded and snipped to make a symmetrical, repetitive design were used as the basis for cutting the cloth. (It is obvious that such a pattern was used for the pieces of this quilt—note especially the symmetry in the borders of the two panels. The two sides of the stylized frond-type leaves are identical, as are the flowers and buds.) Appliques on early quilts were usually made from turkey red, named for the country, not the bird. It was the most common color of fabric available (here even the angel has red wings).

Elite Hawaiian homes of the 19th century adapted the Western custom of the quilting bee. Women gathered together for these social occasions and sat on the floor around low quilting frames. The hostess never quilted; she was responsible for serving an elaborate banquet.

The Beautiful and Unequaled Gardens of Eden and Elenale is attributed to a male quilter. Although, of course, quilts were made almost exclusively by women, there are examples of quilts made by men, among them a Civil War quilt made by a soldier recovering from his war wounds—men's needlework has often been done for therapeutic purposes. President Eisenhower recalled working on a quilt as a boy.

This Adam and Eve quilt incorporates many typical features of the kapa. Its figures are large and dominant, the vegetation lush and tropical. Palm-like leaves border each section of the quilt and are imitated in the angel's wings. Hawaiians placed enormous trust in their national leaders and symbols of royalty were common in quilt designs; here, the crown and similarities to the queen Emma. Although the appliques are not limited to one color or one design, the colors are few, as are the shapes of applique design. The quilting techniques employed are typical echo or contour quilting, which parallel the shape of the applique. In Hawaiian language, it is called "luma lau."

Although designs do not generally prove the geographic derivation of quilts, the Hawaiian quilt is an exception. Quilt types showing strong cultural characteristics usually evolve in areas that are separated culturally or geographically from mainstream America. The Hawaiian islands were separated in both ways, so it is not surprising that a quilt style unique to the locale has developed.

Favorite themes of religion and royalty are combined in this quilt. It is interesting to contemplate Adam and Eve's shame at their nakedness with the native Hawaiian's attitude about nakedness before the arrival of the missionaries. The contrast between the sacred and the secular is apparent in *The Beautiful and Unequaled Gardens.*

The princess of the magic mythical garden, where the tree plays a minor role, is dressed in European-style clothes. She resembles Josephine with her decolletage, hair-do, ribbon at her neck and medallions. She wears the sash of European aristocracy. And Elenale looks like a little Napoleon in his coat with tails, epaulets, striped trousers and shoes with heels. He also carries the medals and braids of the European military. His elaborate crown has a base reminiscent of Napoleon's tricorn. The figures touch; they have a sense of openness and pride. These human beings who dominate the secular/royal side of this two-part creation smile at the world as if they control it.

The serpent, the Tree of Knowledge and the angel dominate the sacred/religious half of the quilt. The rather hefty angel is simply clothed. A hand is raised, as if in blessing, over the beautifully executed tree with its twining serpent that faces Eve. The fearful figures of Adam and Eve are tiny in comparison to the princess and Elenale. They cower and seek to cover themselves as best they can with their hands.

Each world is titled with letters executed in two colors. The solid assertive large shapes and bright colors confirm the supposition that the quilter of this piece was a man. It obviously was someone with artistic talent and a sense of design, as well as commitment to perfection and precision. As previously indicated, this quilt was not made from scraps; it was planned as a work of art. The carefully placed even stitches of the quilting enhance the design, and make this a truly decorative work. They add depth to the floral elements and softness to the red wings of the angel. The beautifully tied, knotted fringe, typical of Hawaiian quilts, is a perfect finishing touch.

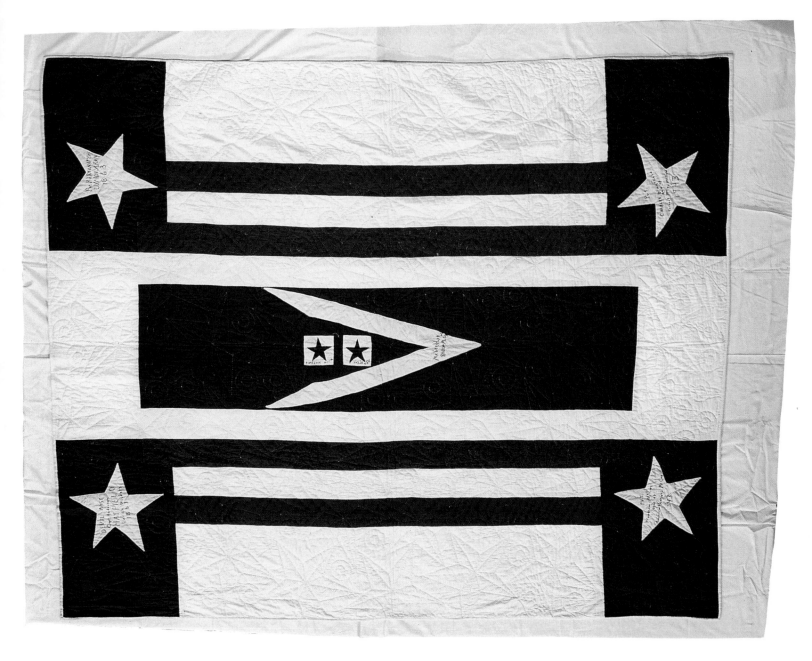

Hatfield-McCoy Victory Quilt.

Hatfield-McCoy Victory Quilt.

CELEBRATIONS

Since the beginning of language and recorded history, poets have taken stylus, quill, or pen in hand to celebrate occasions, places, people, artwork, nations, the seasons, whatever moved them to recreate in words what their imaginations perceived. Individuals, famous and humble, have gained immortality in the body of world literature and in family history through written tributes.

Women, who have made quilts not just out of necessity but for the pleasure of creating something unique as a product of their imaginations, have celebrated a satisfaction in working with fabrics, delighting in colors and bringing order to dozens of bits and pieces. Through quilt making they create things of beauty from an essentially salvage art. Until this century, for most women it was their only means of expression. Women were never really encouraged to write or to paint. For the 19th century woman, and even women today, the "room of one's own" existed, or exists, inside her head squeezed into a small space salvaged from the demands of others' lives. Time for creative fulfillment and concentration only exists between laundry and mending, cooking and a job.

Colonial poet Anne Bradstreet, an exceptional figure for her times, revealed the dim view society took of her writing when she wrote in 1642:

> I am obnoxious to each carping tongue
> Who says my hand a needle better fits. *

It is unthinkable that a woman would have written, as Walt Whitman did in 1855:

> I celebrate myself
>
> I dote on myself—there is that lot of me,
> and all so luscious,
> Each moment, and whatever happens, thrills
> me with joy.
>
> O I am so wonderful!

Just as her time to design a quilt was salvaged from her duties and responsibilities, so were the materials of womans quilts, at first, salvaged from

---

*p. 63, *No Idle Hands: The Social History of Knitting.* Anne L. Macdonald. Ballantine Books, 1988.

the sewing of bed covers and clothing. Still, a woman's quilts were totally hers. In the 19th century they were her only real property, all other goods belonging by law to her husband. In making quilts a woman was free to choose, within the limits of her times and means, the fabric and design. Not encouraged to celebrate herself, or even her family and children, she turned to the world around her for inspiration. She used the quilt as the poet used blank paper, working not in a room alone, but in the center of the household in the art form that fit into her busy life.

Engagements, births, weddings and brides, as the Garden of Eden quilts attested, were celebrated with quilts. Birthdays were celebrated: although it went out of use during the first quarter of the 19th century, the Freedom Quilt commemorated a man's coming of age and was presented to him at a freedom celebration. Friendship was celebrated, the coming of spring, sentiments such as patriotism—whatever caught the quilter's fancy in the world around her could become the focus for a celebration or a tribute in a quilt.

And, although the quilters wouldn't have thought of it, certain quilts celebrated virtues, skills, delights in particular aspects of the surrounding world. Certainly the strip quilts made by Black Americans from strings of salvaged material celebrated thrift. The Amish quilts, with their intricate stitching and amazing color choices, celebrated not just superb needlework but the exuberance of and the quilters' delight in creative activity within the proscribed limitations of the Amish community. The women of Baltimore celebrated a bride and groom in the glorious album quilts, and also the spirit of competition that motivated the superb workmanship of their community of quilters whose work so consistently outshone that of other areas. Two seamstresses from New Jersey celebrated their association with the Great Caruso through his haberdashery quilt! There were, and are, for the tradition continues, as many reasons to pick up scissors and thread as there were and are facets of the American spirit and versions of the American dream. A prize fighter, a financial savior, the world of pop culture, a horse—all were inspirations for quilters to design and fashion a quilt.

Hardly ever were the characteristics of a woman's personality discernible in her quilts, except, of course, when her quilts proved her dedication to the many virtues that kept her household running. There is one exception among the quilts that follow. The Suffrage Quilt is downright subversive for its time, with its scenes of an emancipated woman and a house-husband, complete with apron! Who knows what would have happened to this bold soul if she had dared to put into writing her feelings about woman's place in the world? As it is, her message is disguised behind a more acceptable celebration, the end of the Civil War.

A century ago, women celebrated special moments in their lives by creating a quilt.

HATFIELD-McCOY VICTORY QUILT

Applique and piecework, cotton
By America Hatfield McCoy and Rhoda McCoy
Pike County, Kentucky, 1943
Ohio Historical Society
78 inches by 94 inches

The *Hatfield-McCoy Victory Quilt* celebrates a relationship between families. The feud between the Hatfields and McCoys is as legendary in American popular history as the feud between the Montagues and Capulets in Shakespearean drama. The original clan members lived on the two sides of the Tug Fork of the Big Sandy River which separates West Virginia and Kentucky. Anderson Hatfield and Harmon McCoy held differing loyalties in the Civil War. The initial incident in the blood feud was thought to have been set off by a McCoy accusing a Hatfield of stealing one of his hogs. In 1882 Randolph McCoy's three sons were seized by a squad of Hatfields and brutally murdered. Most of the atrocities in the feud were suffered by the McCoys. In 1888 Kentucky officers killed two Hatfields and captured nine more in a raid. Two of the nine were executed, the others sent to prison. The feud's end was sealed by a wedding joining the two clans in the late 19th century. This patriotic quilt was created in 1943 to celebrate the peace between the two families and recognize the sons of the Hatfield and McCoy clans who served in World War II.

A ballad was written about the making of the quilt which was finished at a quilting bee in Frank McCoy's home at Peter Creek, Kentucky. Women from both families participated. The ballad celebrates the quilt and identifies the names embroidered in the stars—Devil Anse Hatfield and Harmon McCoy—as well as the two young family members fighting in World War II:

I've been down to the quiltin' folks,
A victory quilt, they say;
At Granny Hatfield's old log house
Across on Tadpole Way.
And Rhoda, Bud McCoy's good wife,
With Martha Hatfield, too,
Made up the quilt of calico
With old red, white and blue.
One big star stands for Devil Anse,
Who led the Rebel clan.
Another star—Harmon McCoy,
A faithful Union man.
Woodrow McCoy, another star,
For many victories won,

He was a proud and noble lad,
America Hatfield's son.
The last big star, a Hatfield boy,
Old Tolbert's pride was he,
The small stars, Ace and Anderson,
Who fought across the sea.
This victory quilt to honor them
We'll place within a shrine
With Roosevelt's name and noble deeds
On history's page to shine.

Across the base of the V are the quilters names: Melissa Hatfield and Rhoda McCoy. The names Willie Hatfield and Aga McCoy are embroidered in the upper part of the V.

The quilting is done in a combination of five-pointed stars and circle-within-a-circle.

Star on top at left reads:

DEVIL ANSE
Captain Anderson
Hatfield
Laran Wildcats
1863

Star at bottom on left reads:

Pvt. Woodrow McCoy
son of
America Hatfield McCoy
'43

Star on top at right reads:

Pvt. Harmon McCoy
Union Army
1863

Star at bottom right reads:

Pvt.
Charles D. Hatfield
Tolbout son of
McCoy Hatfield
1943

Farm Scene Quilt.

Farm Scene Quilt.

UNQUILTED SPREAD WITH FARM SCENE

Applique and piecing
By Sarah Ann Gargis
Pennsylvania, 1853
Museum of American Folk Art
Gift of Warner Communications
96 inches by 98 inches

Consisting of a cotton top and muslin backing, this *Farm Scene* quilt has no center stuffing and is not quilted. Either it was intended for use as a summer spread or simply was not finished. Sarah Ann Gargis, whose initials appear on the quilt with the date 1853 (under the right side of the central tree) was celebrating, according to family history, her engagement when she made the quilt.

Her naive style of depicting everyday objects with little reference to traditional art movements qualifies this as a representation of folk art. Nineteenth-century American folk art provides important clues about how life was lived at that time. Rural life, the predominant life style, was obviously a favorite subject of the folk artist. Sarah Gargis can be considered a folk artist as surely as if she had used a paintbrush to create this farm scene.

Typical folk art details are the disregard for scale—note the size of the horses pulling the hand-plow, and size of the flowers relative to trees—and stylizing of objects—note the flowers. The symmetry and balance in geometric pieced quilts and more formal quilts is absent here in the border of flowers and vines.

Farm Scene Quilt.

Pictured in this celebration of rural farm life are scenes of cutting wood, hunting, beekeeping, and plowing. In the center of the quilt a man with a fringe beard, typical of several groups in Pennsylvania, fells a tree with a hatchet, scattering woodchips on the ground about him. Behind him leaning against a split rail fence is an ax and two-man saw. Note also the calico farm wagon with its carefully rendered shape and all the necessary parts, including shaft and footrest. The farm cat keeps the man company while chickens scratch around under an oak tree where a horse waits patiently to be hitched to the wagon and begin hauling away the logs. At the tip top of the tree a gray squirrel nibbles a red acorn in its paws, while another flicks its tail on a lower branch above a monstrous black crow—all everyday details of the Pennsylvania farm scene in the 1850s.

To the right, a man attired in red calico pants and the same fringe beard and hat totes a gun as he and the dog contemplate their prey in its death-bed of stylized grass.

On the opposite side of the central portion of the quilt is a square that depicts the antics of the wildlife in a strawberry patch. Creatures include various birds, chickens, a turtle and a rather large worm or grub on a branch overhanging the berries. The birds all seem to be contemplating the berries while one takes off with a large red berry in its beak.

At top center is the red farmhouse—probably a substantial brick one from its appearance—with three stories. Included in that square with the family dog and cat is a water pump and apple tree with fruit on the branches, but no leaves.

At the bottom is the green barn with pigeons roosting on the roof; a split rail fencing surrounds the barnyard with a horse and cow. The faithfully recorded tools and careful renditions of the solid barn and farmhouse make this quilt an important social document of prosperous life in rural Pennsylvania in the latter part of the last century.

The round beehives used during the last century for beekeeping activities are seen in the upper right corner. Bees flit around while nearby is a cherry tree. In the opposite top corner is the vineyard with green grapes still on the vine and what appears to be a pear tree.

Plowing activities occupy the lower left corner, where a miniscule horse is hitched to a hand plow—note details of the harness. Something is already planted in mounds under poles that have been arranged in teepees to provide a frame for the emerging vines to crawl on. A clutch of three chicks with hen and cock perch near a spade, two-tined fork and wheel barrow. On the other side are stylized plants as well as cattle and a sun that call to mind what Sarah Gargis must have considered important elements of a meadow scene.

Many of the figures in the quilt's border, including the pineapple, a symbol of hospitality and friendship, resemble the stencilled motifs used on furniture, walls and floorcoverings around the time this quilt was made, particularly in the Northeast.

Farm Scene Quilt.

Farm Scene Quilt.

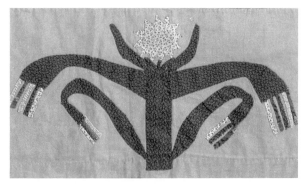

Some are readily identifiable: just above the pineapple is a corn plant; find also the pear tree, sunflower and sycamore leaves with flower—certainly a blossom that fascinates whoever is lucky enough to find one on a spring day.

The red and green used by Sarah Gargis were favorite colors of quilters of her time, and often signified that the quilt containing them was a special occasion one. The orange color of the ground fabric was an unusual choice, and makes the organizational pattern of the quilt quite striking. The play of the square within a square, and diamond within a diamond is intriguing. The whole creation is truly a precise artistic accomplishment of considerable planning, careful cutting and placement. The geometric pieces of the base provide a sharp foil for the folk art details.

Farm Scene Quilt.

Baltimore Album Quilt.

Baltimore Album Quilt.

BALTIMORE ALBUM QUILT

By Hannah Foote
Baltimore, 1850
America Hurrah Antiques, NYC
104 inches square

The *Baltimore Album Quilt,* produced in the Baltimore area during the 1840s and 1850s, combined the best applique techniques with the album design. The album design consisted of separate quilt blocks, usually provided by different individuals, sewn together and signed, to be presented as a testimonial to a person on an anniversary or engagement, or to mark a friendship. A woman leaving a community with her husband to go West or a departing minister's wife might be presented an album quilt as a keepsake or remembrance. Both men and women signed the quilts' blocks, the women in embroidery, the men in ink. Although usually a group endeavor, sometimes album quilts were made by one quilter, a fact determined by the uniformity of workmanship on the quilt. After the middle of the 19th century, autograph quilts, made by one woman who asked her friends to sign the blocks, became popular, based on the autograph album craze. Family album quilts were a version that had family members' names embroidered on the blocks.

The Baltimore quilts were marked by unusual designs and excellent workmanship. Piecework was often used in sashings and borders, but it is the remarkable applique, which reached its zenith in these quilts, that they are celebrated for. The quilts are a triumph of creative talent and highflown sentiments such as love, reverence, patriotism and friendship. Red and green fabrics dominate in mo-

tifs using wreaths, flowers, baskets, lyres, laurels, fruits, monuments from the city of Baltimore, and religious and patriotic symbols. Also common are hearts, figures of men, women and children, and pictorial blocks, that exude naive charm and even humor.

The eagle (second row) was a favorite symbol of all quilters. Although it was opposed as a national symbol by Benjamin Franklin, who dubbed it a bird of "bad moral character," the eagle had been incorporated into the Great Seal of the United States. In *American Quilts and Coverlets,* Florence Peto wrote, "From the Federal Period to the Centennial in 1876 no craftsman felt more of a possessive attitude towards the emblem of freedom than the American quilter,"* proceeding to cite the eagle's increased use in quilt making whenever war loomed and noting that the British textile industry had produced eagle prints expressly for export to America.

Album quilts were often made as bridal quilts. Because they were saved for best, unlike the much-used plainer quilts, many have survived, stirring up interest as to why they are so uniformly superior. In general the making of album quilts encouraged competition among the quilters that resulted in fine products. But the Baltimore quilts are so unique that the best of them are thought to have been made by one woman, a professional quilter named Mary Evans Ford. A bricklayer's daughter, she, like one-third of the Baltimore population who were Methodist, attended church sewing circles and religious classes. She resided in the same parish with other definitely identified quilt makers. Although most of the Baltimore quilts are signed, her signature is not on any quilt. It is surmised, therefore (partly because of a revealing quilt block found by her greatnephew in 1973), that she designed and sewed blocks which were then sold and inscribed by others.

The Baltimore quilt lost popularity in the early 1850s when other fads, such as china painting and tatting, took its place. In 1857 an economic downturn put an end to the leisurely way of life that had produced the quilts. Prior to this, a split in the Methodist Church over the slavery issue in 1844 undermined church solidarity and with it church-centered activities that were important to the production of quilts. (The church dissension mirrored opinions throughout Maryland, which entered the Civil War tragically divided.)

This Hannah Foote quilt, thought to have been made in celebration of a marriage, exhibits many of Mary Evans Ford's trademarks. The majority of the blocks are credited to her. Signs of her workmanship include:

  —Delicately woven baskets with flared rims—two in the second row, both with considerable details and smooth edges on concave and convex curves; great skill in careful placement of each strip of fabric
  —triple bowknots on wreaths in second and third rows, an unusual configuration for a bow, but one that adds nice balance to the base of a wreath
  —shaded fabrics indicating contours of animals and people; evident in this quilt in the blue and brown fabrics. Careful consideration has been used in cutting the pieces so that the shadings in the cloth add depth of the blooms. Often the

*p. 30, *American Quilts and Coverlets.* Florence Peto. Chanticleer Press, New York, 1949.

darkest band is used in the center of the petal, or sometimes on one-half of a bud. Note how effectively it has been used in the attire of the gardener in the third row. It is also used to advantage in the depiction of the chain on the anchor in the fourth row making it appear to twist.

Features typical of Baltimore album quilts in general are:

—stylized flowers and leaves
—ink-drawn features, now badly faded, on the sailor in bottom row
—white roses, a particular symbol of Mary Evans Ford for herself, occurring in eight of the blocks in this quilt
—baskets and urns holding flowers
—wreaths of all shapes, including the lyre-shaped wreaths related to the sacred harp of religious symbolism and laurel wreaths
—the Bible, here in a basket of flowers in the second row
—the anchor, symbol of hope, as well as pertinent to Baltimore's being a busy port city; the sailor also was representative of a large group in the Baltimore population
—pictorial blocks of charming scenes, frolicking dogs and light-hearted creatures.

The two pictorial blocks in Hannah Foote's quilt have many similarities, although the pastoral scene in the center is far less complex than the other scene in the same row, which causes the observer to wonder if they were indeed made by the same person. As previously noted the variegated fabric is not used to its best advantage in this block. The basic shapes in the foliage are the same. However

the appearance of the trees is considerably different because the centerpiece trees are done in a combination of plain green and calico fabric while the others employ variegated greens and a print or embroidered fabric with scroll-like designs. Although the two ducks and little dog, at first glance, seem identical, they were not at least cut from the same pattern, those in the central panel being far stockier.

The village scene is much more ambitious. The young lady, as she strolls past a bountiful garden of flowers behind an elaborate white plank fence, has still more blossoms on her bonnet with pink ribbons. She wears a full jacket that spreads over her tucked skirts above pantaloons. Over her arm is a carefully shaped basket with flared top. Rightly so, the costume of the milk-maid is simpler. But in a world where most quilts have the most elaborate square in the center, this is unusual.

In addition to the applique, there are embroidery accents on this quilt. They are evident in the petals of the more ambitious baskets of flowers. Embroidery is also used to fabricate tendrils and delicate foliage around some of the buds. The urn under the anchor at the bottom has considerable stitchery embellishment. And, of course, the sailor teasing the little dog by holding the red apples out of reach has embroidery as do the stylized bird and butterfly in the block next to this.

In addition to the white of the background, only one other fabric is used in the borders, a red and gold small print. This is carefully cut and appliqued in a stairstep configuration which really works on only one of the four corners—in the other three, it does not come together correctly. The quilting in diagonal rows disappears into the background.

Afro-American "Baltimore Album" Quilt.

Afro-American "Baltimore Album" Quilt.

AFRO-AMERICAN "BALTIMORE ALBUM" QUILT

1915–1920
America Hurrah Antiques, NYC
64 inches by 74 inches

The unusual *Afro-American "Baltimore Album" Quilt* was certainly made by a black quilter who had seen a Baltimore quilt, from which she adapted familiar motifs. The quilt is crammed with the quilter's naive versions of baskets and urns, wreaths, stylized flowers, hearts and birds, all of which figure frequently in Baltimore quilt designs.

Several features of the quilt place it as definitely the work of a Black quilter. The first is the strip added to the right side of the quilt to even out the quilt's measurements. Strip, or string, quilts in which long narrow strips were the basic unit of the quilt, were the most popular type of Afro-Ameri-

can pieced quilts. Unmeasured piecing, once thought to be mistakes, was a mark of such quilts, as it is of this one. The lack of attention to precise measurement, so important in traditional pieced quilts, gives these quilts a quality of spontaneity, the feeling that they have been put together by accident more than by design.

Several superstitions are connected with this custom of "accidental" piecing. One is an African belief that every time there was a break in the pattern it meant a rebirth of ancestral power in the artisan working on an object. Another, subscribed to by superstitious white quilters as well, who often

Afro-American "Baltimore Album" Quilt.

purposely sewed an irregular piece into a pattern, or left a quilting design unfinished, is that including an imperfection wards off evil spirits and keeps the quilter humble. There could be no question that the quilter was not aiming at the perfection only God can achieve. So, many quilters had beliefs that permitted them to completely disregard any necessity to finish a quilt in fabric that matched any other part of the quilt.

Afro-American quilters also believed that shades of adjacent pieces should not be too closely related or they would fight each other—thus the stark contrasts, with no subtleties of color in this quilt.

Unlike its Baltimore prototype, this quilt has no graphic elements—no borders or sashings. The quilt is not done up in readily defined blocks. The blocks in the background are visible, but often the designs spread over the edges, indicating that the blocks of the background were sewn together prior to the applique of some parts of the designs. This could be the result of yet another superstition: evil spirits follow straight lines. Afro-American art, with curvy, crooked lines, gives the wicked ones no chance.

Two major features of the Afro-American quilt

suggest its maker came from the West Indies. The figures at the top, done in relief, resemble dolls from the islands of Trinidad and Tobago. Also, the quilt's center, with cross and angels, is a primitive interpretation of Christian motifs.

The central motif of the quilt is the one single unit that exists as a clearly defined entity. It is contained within four squares set slightly off the center of the quilt. In each corner is a red-haired angel, with light complexion, embroidered face and pink blushing cheeks. All wear pearl necklaces. Those on the left have wings heavily outlined in green while those on the right are done in red. The rest of the square is filled with an undulating wreath, the vine of which stands out in its dark green and red colors more than does the foliage. The six-petalled red blooms are attached to the vine with slim calico stems. The flowers on the outside have tan calico centers while those on the interior have dark calico centers. The leaves on the outside of the wreath are in tan while those in the center are in a variety of colors. The two figures on either side of the cross resemble the angels in the corners with the red hair, stitched features and blushing cheeks. They also wear pearls. Their white gowns are gathered at the waist and have full sleeves. When the quilt was new, they must have been quite three-dimensional.

The dolls at the top, closely resembling dolls made in the islands of Trinidad and Tobago in the West Indies, suggest the quilter was originally from that area. The rose dress of the woman has a large lace portrait collar with wide bands of lace on the skirt and the sleeves. She has a soft pink bow at her neckline and wears a hat. He sports a full blue and white stripped shirt with cording details at the neck and shoulders. Black trousers and buttoned shoes complete his costume. While she carries a basket, he has a package tied with string. At her feet is a velvet bench or divan with rolled bolsters and a silk ruffle.

It is interesting to compare some of the motifs with those in a Baltimore quilt. An attempt has been made to duplicate an intricately scrolled basket at upper left. The strips cross haphazardly and are of uneven widths. Instead of being gracefully arranged with curving stems over the side of the basket, the flowers seem to have stalks that have been broken by the edge of the container.

Below this block is a square that seems to have a carefully measured and accurately cut and laid down applique of four white flowers with red centers and red and blue leaves. On comparison, however, the flowers are not accurately cut from a pattern.

Continuing down the same side is a cock with comb and fabulous tail—perhaps an attempt at a peacock or bird of paradise. Below this is another floral arrangement, this one in an urn of imaginative dimensions. Again a bloom spills out of the container on each side.

The bottom square is a crude rendition of a wreath of red flowers on a blue vine—it is far from round. At its center is a three-dimensional rosette made from several pieces of gathered fabric with a red pouf for a center. At the opposite bottom corner is a more carefully executed red-flowered wreath. Moving up that side above the bird is a large rectangular block covered with floral patches in a random arrangement. Other designs resemble those done by women belonging to the establishment—note especially the two-color buds on the wreath next to the male doll.

Whoever the Black woman was who created this quilt, she must have found considerable pleasure and amusement in its construction and a wonderful diversion from her daily hours filled with menial chores.

Afro-American "Baltimore Album" Quilt.

Suffrage Album Quilt.

Suffrage Album Quilt.

SUFFRAGE ALBUM QUILT

Applique, reverse applique and embroidery
Chicago area, c.1860–1880
Collection of Dr. and Mrs. John Livingston
and Mrs. Elizabeth Livingston Jaeger
70 inches by 69 inches

The *Suffrage Album Quilt*, made just a few years after the 1848 United States Women's Convention in Seneca Falls, New York, is a unique quilt, created by a woman of unusual imagination and foresight. It contains scenes of a woman doing things considered shocking at the time: leaving the house where her husband wearing an apron stays behind; driving her own buggy; and, worst of all, speaking at a meeting. In 1837 a woman speaking at a meeting in Philadelphia caused a riot! In 1853 the Reverend D. Matthews, in his "Letter to School Girls," inveighed against "those females who deliver public haranges and desire to be heard in

legislative halls and political contests who are like the meteors that blaze across the sky, and disappear. God made women for domestic duties, and her nature must be very much perverted before she can cease to love such duties."[*]

The linking of quilt making and women's rights was a common jumping-off place for women's rights advocates. The authors of *Hearts and Hands* quote Abigal Duniway of Oregon, who called quilts "primary symbols of women's unpaid subjection."[**] In

[*]p. 54, *No Idle Hands.*

[**]p. 94, *Hearts and Hands.*

57

response to society's insistence that women be valued only for domestic skills, Maria Mitchell, a noted astronomer and the first woman to be admitted to the American Academy of Arts and Sciences, wrote in her diary: "It seems to me that the needle is the chain of woman, and has fettered her more than the laws of the country."****

Made after the end of the Civil War, this quilt celebrates freedom, as symbolized, according to the notes, by the deer under the oak tree. By implication, of course, it celebrates not simply the end of

Techniques employed in the quilt are applique, embroidery and reverse applique. Reverse applique, also called in-laid applique, is not commonly found in antique quilts but is used frequently in Central and South American needlework. It is achieved by cutting the design out of (rather than sewing it

onto) the top piece. Then tiny hems are clipped and turned underneath along the inside of the pattern holes, and the piece is then applied to a background piece of a contrasting color. Here the feather shapes in the border are done with this technique. The quilt is quilted overall with echo, or contour, quilting following shapes in the design. the war—but the freedom of the slaves. Less subtly, it defiantly speaks out for women's freedom to realize herself outside of the home.

It's possible that the pantaloons worn by the school marm are further evidence of the quilter's defiance of convention. Historians studying the quilt have speculated about the omission of an explanation for the twelfth block, where a little girl is praying in a chapel. Since fabrics used in the block do not appear elsewhere in the quilt, it has

***p. 55, *No Idle Hands.*

Details from the Suffrage Album Quilt.

been proposed that perhaps the quilter, who may have been the child's mother, has died, and the little girl is praying for her. It could be, though, that the little girl, following her mother's lead, is praying for freedom for women from subjugation in the home.

The *Suffrage Album* is composed of twenty-five blocks, the standard unit of album quilts; some contain bordered blocks with flower and fruit designs; others, circles in which parts of a story are related. When this quilt's present owner received the quilt, a tag was pinned to each of the story blocks with the following descriptions:

Story of Woman's Rights Quilt in pictures.

Made over 100 years ago.

1. Man is in kitchen doing dishes. He is owlish and cross. Represented by owls.*
2. The woman has gone to lecture on Woman's Rights. How important she is driving.
3. She is lecturing to all men only 1 woman and that is her Pal.
4. She was told that war has been declared and she comes home and tell(s) her husband he will have to go to war.

5. She gets him all ready to go to war and now he is telling her if God spares his life he will return.
6. He does return and this is their meeting.

   This is all of the story but in order to fill in the quilt there is other pictures.

7. The deer under the oak represents freedom.
8. Ravens are bringing food to the Grandmother and she is giving cake to the Grandchild.
9. Angels are guarding the Blind Man and His Dog. Notice how he is groping his way.
10. The School Marm is wondering what is the matter with the Pupil. He can't get the problem on his slate.
11. Is the soldiers under the Flag of Freedom.

*Every other block is birds, fruit and flowers. Notice fine stitches and also how the border is made.

There is not another quilt like this.

Chester Dare Quilt.

Chester Dare Quilt.

CHESTER DARE QUILT

Wool, velvet, and heavy cotton with silk embroidery
By Annie Hines Miller
Kentucky, 1877
Kentucky Museum, Western Kentucky University
79 inches by 84 inches

Annie Miller's *Chester Dare Quilt* celebrates the great Kentucky bay stallion Chester Dare, produced in 1882 from a line of distinguished ancestors in the tradition of the great Kentucky racehorses that have made the Kentucky Derby a world-class equine event. Chester Dare was prominent in Kentucky saddle horse circles until his death in 1904.

The *Chester Dare Quilt* is a rather homey and unsophisticated version of the crazy quilt style. Made in rural Kentucky, it is composed mostly of cottons and woolens, although the horse's portrait is velvet, as is the dark border, which typically sets off the design as a frame does a painting. The sixteen squares, each composed of asymmetrical patches, are embroidered in a simple outline stitch with motifs popular in the crazy quilt style. In keeping with the asymmetrical mood of the quilt, the portrait of the horse is off center. Like an artist who displays his preliminary sketches with the finished painting, Mrs. Miller's sketches for the portrait are shown in the area diagonal to it. Her signature, Annie Miller, is above the horse.

Legend has it that hairs from Chester Dare's tail were taken by riverboat to New Orleans to match to velvet appropriate for his portrait. Family history relates that Annie Miller's husband, who was much older than she was, was extremely jealous and kept her at home when he was out. This may account for her taking the time to make the quilt. (Later in the crazy quilt craze, *Harper's Bazaar* estimated it took 1500 hours to make a quilt.) At any rate, in order to assure himself that his wife would remain at home, Mr. Miller supposedly carried Annie's shoes with when he left the house. Once she decided to visit her mother's neighboring farm and walked barefoot through the snow. Her death at 26 is believed to have been caused by pneumonia contracted on that walk.

Although Chester Dare is done in velvet, as are many of the patches and the border, the quilt contains some very coarse and homespun fabrics: shirt plaids, houndstooth check, dress prints and stripes. There is a rainbow of color in the floss used and a beautiful sampling of skill in the embroidery stitches. The horse is simply done with a rust outline that catches the lighter undertones in the stallion's coat. He has white embroidered hoofs and a black mane and tail done with thousands of closely packed stitches that show off the sheen of a tail groomed to perfection.

The motifs embroidered on the patches are myriad and probably many had special associations for the quilter:

pansies	lilies	cat
daisies	asters	stars
rabbits	roses	owls
violets	morning glories	grapes
clover	children	cherries
horses	iris	fuchia
butterflies	daffodils	a cow
swans	a fat sow	swans

All of the above are skillfully executed, but the stitches that truly deserve careful scrutinization are those outlining the hundreds of patches. Their tremendous variety and meticulous rendering make the quilt an apt testimony to the skill of the seamstress.

The Crazy Quilt

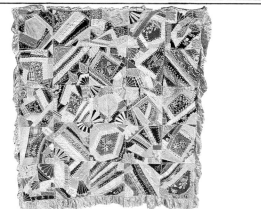

The most popular quilt type by far during the last third of the 19th century was the crazy quilt. By then the more cosmopolitan women were abandoning the familiar patchwork quilt to those who lived in rural areas. Preferring storebought counterpanes and bedcovers, they were ready for new challenges to their needles.

As America's centennial year approached, women were beginning to accept responsibility for decorating the home and making it a beautiful retreat from the outside world. The Aesthetic Era, when design became a factor often outshining utility, was upon the horizon for settled women of leisure.

Among the exhibits at the 1886 Centennial in Philadelphia were needlework displays from England, featuring fancy embroidery stitches, and from Japan, where patterns of assymetrical designs decorated art objects. The imaginations of needlewomen among the almost 10 million who attended the Centennial were seized. *Harper's Bazaar* magazine wrote that geometric quilts were out. Women now preferred quilts "more like the changing figures of the kaleidescope, or the beauty and infinite variety of Oriental mosaics." These new quilts were called "Japanese silks," or embroidered quilts. They were constructed on the same plan as quilts of the Log Cabin design, a popular traditional quilt pattern which in the '70s women sometimes made from silks. Unlike the pieced quilt, the Log Cabin quilt was assembled by stitching strips of fabric—logs—around a starter, or center piece, which had been sewed to a foundation block of muslin. Instead of logs, the crazy quilt used odd-shaped scraps of silks, velvet and ribbons randomly placed on blocks. Connecting seams were disguised with feather or other fancy stitching.

Mormon Trail Quilt.

MORMON TRAIL QUILT

Patchwork and applique with embroidery, c. 1880
By Agnes Bell Cunningham
Fremont Pioneer Museum, Wyoming
Photographed by Lorin Just

Another example of a crazy quilt is the *Mormon Trail Quilt* made by Agnes Bell Cunningham, c. 1880, allegedly from scraps collected on a trip west. This impressive work is comprised of 25 squares, only some of which contain such embroidered motifs as:

elk	clover
sunburst	leaves
thistles	anemonies
poppy	dragonfly
horseshoe	stylized flowers
woman doing laundry	

Many squares are composed of ribbons and several have corners embellished with an assortment of fans. There is one in each corner of the center square as well as the corners that butt up against it, making for a center of interest. The embroidery is done primarily with gold floss, although some pink is evident. The assemblage of stitches laying down the edges of the patches is impressive, and deserving of careful appreciation.

The quilt is finished with a red silk ruffle now in a state of severe disintegration. It originally had a gold edging and was embroidered with tiny floral sprays. When it was in better condition, it must have presented a dazzling display of ostentacious taste wherever it was used.

John L. Sullivan Crazy Quilt.

John L. Sullivan Crazy Quilt.

JOHN L. SULLIVAN CRAZY QUILT

Silk and velvet, embroidery
Illinois, 1888
America Hurrah Antiques, NYC
79 inches by 76 inches

The date on the *John L. Sullivan Crazy Quilt* indicates it was created at the height of the crazy quilt mania, when it was an aim of many fashionable young males to own one: undoubtedly, this one was made for a man. Typical of the spirit of its oversentimental times, the amount of work it displays explains why some joked that the name "crazy quilt" meant you had to be crazy to make one, or it drove you crazy if you did. It was proof in the parlor that the woman of leisure had been released by Sears Roebuck from the production of utilitarian bedding to follow her own frivolous needlework pursuits.

Born in 1858, John L. Sullivan began his fighting career in a Boston theater, knocking his opponent

into the orchestra with his first blow. He developed a reputation for hitting hard enough to "knock a horse down." In 1882 he became American heavyweight champion by knocking out Paddy Ryan bareknuckled in the ninth round. Known as the "Boston Strong Boy," he became a popular idol. His method of fighting was simply to hammer his opponent into unconsciousness.

Sullivan's hazel eyes, burning black with fury—effectively portrayed in his embroidered hairy-chested likeness on the quilt—seemed to paralyze his opponents. He lived a riotous life, but could knock out his opponent no matter what shape he was in. Flamboyantly patriotic, he hated "foreign fighters." Englishman Charlie Mitchell actually

65

knocked Sullivan down in a fight but later the police had to be called in to save Mitchell's life. In 1888 Sullivan went abroad to meet the Prince of Wales and fight Mitchell on Baron Rothschild's estate in France. Much to Sullivan's chagrin, the fight was declared a draw after three hours and both fighters were arrested.

In 1889 Sullivan was a wreck from dissipation but he trained into condition and retained the championship, fighting Jake Kilrain in boxing's last bareknuckled fight. In 1892 James Corbett snatched the crown from him in the twenty-first round of a challenge fight.

Sullivan had wasted his fortune, including the $10,000 diamond-studded belt given him by Boston city officials. He took to the stage, toured in vaudeville, opened a bar in New York and a saloon in Boston. In 1905 Sullivan reformed and became a temperance lecturer. Twice-married, he died in poverty on a farm in Massachusetts where he lived with a former sparring partner named George Bush.

The *Sullivan Crazy Quilt*, made of scraps of silk, velvet and ribbon put together and decorated according to the crazy quilt directive to use "any old design," is an apt mirror for the boxer's riotous life

style. Made just before his fight with Kilrain, it includes an outline portrait of two boxers (just below Sullivan). Obviously created in the Chicago area, it contains names of many Chicago papers—*The Sunday Herald, Police Gazette, Daily News, Tribune*—and bits of newspaper headlines: "Bloody Butchery," "Bankrupt," "Who Killed Mr. Cronin?" as well as weather reports, all of them stressing Chicago's climate: "c-o-l-d!"

John L. Sullivan Crazy Quilt.

Besides newspaper items, there are advertisements with drawings of corsets, "holiday slippers," and names of products—Puritan Silks, Jolly Tar Tobacco; and services—Mr. Jacob's Academy of Music; and even what appears to be a public service notice—a drawing of a dog wearing a muzzle with "For the Sake of the Public" embroidered below. There are horseshoes with "good luck" written on them, names of Chicago districts—Haymarket and The Hub—and slogans for unidentified products: "Always the cheapest, never too cheap." And the line from a hymn: "They come, Father Abraham, 100,000 strong."

John L. Sullivan Crazy Quilt.

Next to this hodgepodge of data and pictures, embroidered on odd-shaped pieces arranged into rectangles which frame the Sullivan portrait, is a rectangle on the right side done in the traditional Ninepatch design, a fundamental block construction in quilt making based on the repetition of one square nine times, in any variety of fabrics. (Amish quilts employ many variations of the Ninepatch.) Two sections above the Ninepatch are relatively undecorated, as is one at the top center of the quilt. It appears as though the ambitious quilter ran out of steam.

Whereas many crazy quilts were used as a background against which to display embroidery skills, relatively few such skills embellish the Sullivan quilt. The vast majority of the patches are edged with cross stitching, and there is some herringbone and feather stitching. Even the ribbon stripes joined in the lower left are brought together with cross stitches. There are beautiful examples of a very smoothly executed satin stitch in the headlines, as well as nice outlining and backstitching in the cartoons. A border of plush and velvet frames the quilt.

John L. Sullivan Crazy Quilt.

Mrs. White's Folk Art Quilt.

Mrs. White's Folk Art Quilt.

MRS. WHITE'S FOLK ART QUILT

Pictorial applique
By Mrs. Cecil White
Hartford, Connecticut
America Hurrah Antiques, NYC
77 inches by 66 inches

A lively celebration of popular culture, *Mrs. White's Folk Art Quilt* might be called a '20s pop art quilt. Appliqued of plain, everyday fabrics, primarily by machine and rather casually, it contains blatant stereotypes of minorities, figures from comic strips of the time, stock situations that were the subject of slapstick—all strung together in a way that achieves the effect of an animated film. It qualifies as folk art in that the artist, a Mrs. Cecil White from Hartford, used material at hand, and she has interpreted the popular culture with no regard for fine arts considerations of technique, materials, or content.

Among the standard slapstick subjects in the quilt are a drunk leaning against a lamppost sharing a joke with his buddy in black pants and a blue plaid shirt, two women in full-skirted dresses screeching from atop a chair and footstool at the two mice below them, a man preparing to throw a shoe at three cats sitting on a fence under the moon and stars, a hobo contemplating the comforts of a dog in his house while two geese spar in the foreground and an ostrich stands behind, a dog biting the seat of a man's pants as he runs away from a woman yelling at him, and a fast-moving curly-tailed dog, or pig, upsetting a man.

Comic strips of the period include Barney Google (three squares down, and three squares over) with the bucking horse wearing blinders, and Maggie and Jiggs (five squares down, and four over) with Jiggs sneaking by Maggie with a bag over his head.

Typical scenes from American life are a street sweeper, men playing golf (a new sport at the time—note the plus-four knickers on the man), football players, three fishermen angling for three fish, men standing at a bar with mugs of beer in front of them, the one on the end is handing a bill to the bartender who is serving another mug.

Children play in a wheelbarrow, and four women dance in a circle to the tune of a violin played by a man in a striped shirt and brown checked pants.

Mrs. White's Folk Art Quilt.

There is a boxing match with the referee counting as a man goes down. A bootblack shines a man's shoes, a cowboy swings his lariat and two Indians in fringed buckskin dance with headdresses and a tomahawk. Black men face each other across a checker game, chorus girls dance, and a porter carrying a bag hails a taxi(?) for a woman in a pink hat and purple cape. An elegantly dressed man with a walking stick strolls with a woman complete with brimmed hat and pocketbook. A sailor and doughboy salute and tennis players greet each other over a brown mesh net. Pocahontas and a brave paddle canoes on rather frayed water under the moon. A trolley car with a cable has faces of people in the windows, a Romeo on a ladder kisses a girl in a window between a pair of gigantic flowers over which a bird hovers. A policeman with a huge belly chases a robber; two men shoot pool, and a lady pushes a baby carriage. Two buxom bathing beauties appear ready to jump in the water, and a woman with a fancy hair-do and beads poses for a

Mrs. White's Folk Art Quilt.

Mrs. White's Folk Art Quilt.

portrait painter who has a palette, brush, paints, and wears a smock with a kerchief around his neck. Not to be missed is the wedding scene at left center bottom row. A pastor blesses the bride in long veil with a bouquet and a groom with a ribbon stripe down the side of his trousers.

The manner in which ethnic groups are portrayed would bring charges of racism and prejudice today. A Chinaman with slanted eyes and pigtail is doing ironing, and Blacks are depicted in an especially degrading way. Particularly curious are the scenes of mixed races: a doctor and a nurse, a couple playing tennis, and most surprising, a couple dancing. The dark man in the dancing couple may be the stereotypical Latin lover, or his dark skin may be due only to the fact that the seamstress used whatever fabrics she had on hand.

Among features that helped in dating the quilt are the uniforms of the two servicemen, and the cars around the border of the quilt. In research done on the quilt, it was ascertained that two Mrs. Cecil Whites lived in Hartford at the time, one in a racially mixed neighborhood. Since the characters and scenes in the quilt are all stereotypes, it's unlikely she imposed any life experiences of her own, but merely utilized her powers of observation—and appreciation—of popular culture.

The trains, cars, and trucks around the black border date to the late teens and twenties. The trains are rather crudely cut with frayed edges and decoration done by machine. The trucks in the left margin are in two colors and show more extensive detailing as do the cars on the opposite side. Note that all varieties of cars are present: limousines to family cars and sportsters.

All types of sporty and homespun fabrics are used in this quilt: shirt plaids, denims, chambray, and a few pieces of dress and drapery fabrics. Strips

of the black background separate the blocks with red fabric rosettes attached with embroidery floss.

The observer is first attracted to the central square which is double the size of the others. It is very possible this indicates the quilter lived on a farm. The farmer in checked overalls and a straw hat draws water from a well in the midst of pigs, chickens, a horse and cow, plus duck, while a boy in blue overalls and a red-striped shirt teases a cat with a toy.

This folk art quilt does in ways appear rather crude. The sewing machine (patented in 1846 by Elias Howe, Jr.) was seldom used in applique, and this quilt proves why: clumsily applied, the figures are badly frayed. But this is an extremely ambitious project, and one, no doubt, that provided many hours of amusement for the seamstress, as it still provides considerable entertainment for the person who is willing to give it a careful examination today.

Mrs. White's Folk Art Quilt.

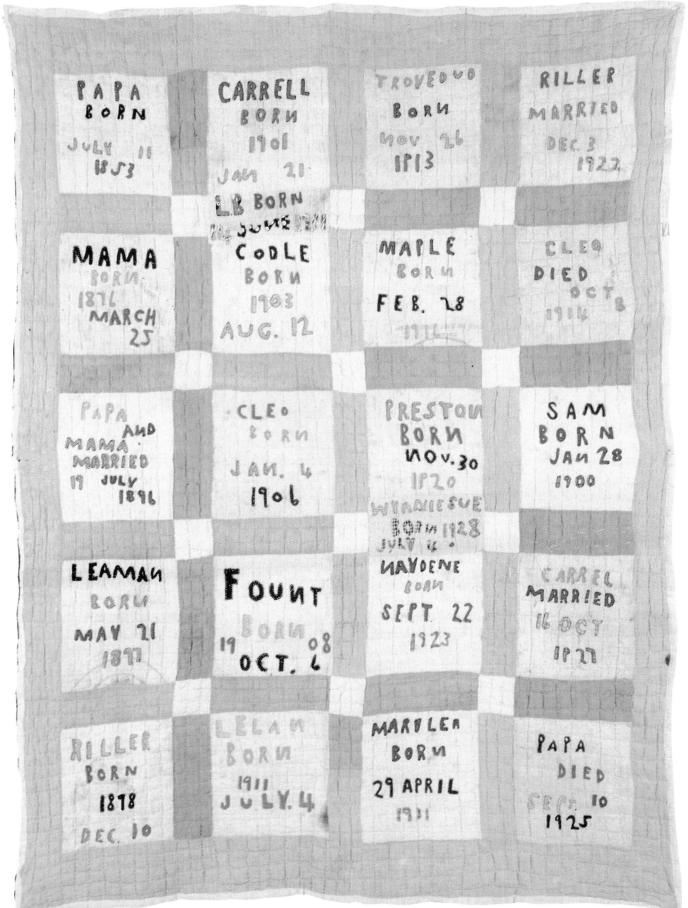

Texas Geneology Quilt.

Texas Geneology Quilt.

TEXAS GENEOLOGY QUILT

Piecing and applique
By Susa Hale Harris
Hunt County, Texas, c. 1927
Laura Fisher/antique quilts & Americana
61 inches by 80 inches

Susa Harris pieced and appliqued the *Texas Geneology Quilt.* She had eleven children between 1897 and 1923. After she died, her son Troy Harris said, "They were farmers and my momma loved to make quilts. When she died I bet there were 100 quilts in a big old quilt box."

The Harrises were poor and uneducated, and lived in rural Texas, a predominantly rural state until the recent past. Mrs. Harris probably could not have found manufactured fabrics for her quilts even if she'd been able to afford them. Poor rural women had to make do with what they could find. Burlap feed bags were often used for stuffing a quilt, and printed flour sacks for a top and bottom.

Faintly discernible on one of the white blocks of the quilt's top, and on the back, are logos from two milling companies

Eagle Mill & Co.
The Quality Miller, Oklahoma

and

Harvest Queen Mill & Elev. Co.
"Every sack guaranteed"

It is unusual that a quilt made by a poor white farm woman has survived. The quilt box of Susa Harris turned up at a flea market. The very family she had celebrated in her crudely assembled quilt with names lovingly, if awkwardly, appliqued with a blanket stitch in the order determined by their date of birth, had not even unfolded the quilts when they put them up for sale.

This quilt is likewise unique in that family tree quilts are very rare; usually needlework samplers were the means of tracing family histories. Mrs. Harris also recorded her family's birth, death and marriage dates in the family Bible, as did many other families.

Much can be learned about the Harris family and life in rural Texas early in the century. Names given to the children were sometimes invented, the spelling obviously figured out phonetically and often spelled two different ways, with backwards crude letter shapes.

Examining the blocks down the left side of the quilt and doing some arithmetic, the fact is obvious that papa was 22 years older than mama when they were married in July of 1896—no doubt an earlier wife had succumbed to the rigors of Texas rural life. So, a man already in his forties had a twenty-year-old bride. Eight months after their marriage Leaman arrived; less than two years later, Riller, and then Carrell. Codle, Cleo, Fount, Lelan, Troveound, Maples, Preston and Naydene followed in rapid succession, only towards the end being born more than two years apart. Wynnie Sue (a grandson, according to his Uncle Troy) and L. B.,

Details from the Texas Geneology Quilt.

another grandson, have been added between other blocks. On studying the location of some of the other children, one can see that they are also out of their birth order—it must have been difficult to keep it all straight.

In the righthand column is recorded the marriage of Riller in December 1922. He would have been twenty-four years old. Cleo died in 1914 when she would have been only eight, and Carrel also was married—she was 26 if it refers to the same person as that spelled "Carrell" whose birth was recorded as 1901 at the top of the second column. In the end papa died in 1925 at the age of 72, not too long after his last child was born, and leaving a wife of 49. What a life! If Susa Harris did in truth leave 100 quilts, one wonders when she had time to make them.

The bright white squares of this quilt with their multi-colored and crudely cut letters stand out against the cream and tan background. Some of the horizontal and vertical bars between the squares are darker than the background. The quilting is done in parallel lines forming squares. Although Susa Harris surely did not have much time for artistic pursuits, she did have some artistic sense. Proportionately, the square white quilt blocks are balanced, nicely with the smaller white squares where the bars cross, and the whole is pulled together by the square pattern in the quilting.

Details from the Texas Geneology Quilt.

Townsend Recovery Plan Quilt.

*Townsend Recovery
Plan Quilt.*

TOWNSEND RECOVERY PLAN QUILT

Piecing and embroidery, with applique center
South Dakota, 1934–35
America Hurrah Antiques, NYC
96 inches by 92 inches

The eighty-block *Townsend Recovery Plan Quilt* was pieced to promote the Old-Age Revolving Pension Plan announced by Dr. Francis E. Townsend on January 1, 1934, considered to be the salvation by many who had been hurt financially after the panic of 1929. One of several economic movements aimed at assisting victims of the Great Depression, it proposed that everyone over 60, who was not working, would receive $200 a month in scrip, (paper money) to be spent in the United States within the month it was received, or five days thereafter.

Townsend argued that his plan was "all we need to create a stabilized prosperity throughout the country. With the scrip in circulation as money, businesses would be encouraged to reopen and unemployment would end," he said. Although eventually condemned by Congress as unsound, the Townsend Plan at first appeared to be the salvation of many of its adherents. Townsend Clubs, their numbers reaching 2½ million, were organized to support the idea. Dr. Townsend's ideas carried into the old age elements of the Social Security Act of 1935. Townsend was eventually investigated by Congress and cited for contempt when he stalked out of the hearing. In 1936 he tried his hand at unseating F.D.R. by running with the radio priest Dr. Coughlin under the banner of the Union Party, which Coughlin had helped found in 1934.

This quilt was embroidered in Mitchell, South Dakota, by members of small businesses who believed in Dr. Townsend's plan. Each block has a flower-like embroidered shape with the name of the business in the center and the names of the employees on the petals. It is interesting to note what the varying organizations did with the basic flower shape. Many include an advertisement slogan, in hopes of attracting some business. Some even include a telephone number. Two names may be written across two petals, or three across three—apparently those doing the needlework found that they had a more workable space that way. Each employee was responsible for a petal in some businesses, and others had a selected needlewoman do it all, as on the lower left: "Geo. A. Tobin Transfer, Phone 9332." Others just had their most talented seamstress put the block together.

Also embroidered on the quilt are mottoes celebrating the Townsend Plan and its goals:

—Townsend Plan pays as it goes, eliminating cost & shame of the pauper system.
—In God, not Greed we trust.
—A Nation is known for its treatment of Youth and its Aged.
—America's pauper system is disrespect for its aged and therefore pagan.
—God decrees Youth for work, Age for Leisure—Townsend
—Some are too busy to be wise, others too wise to be busy—J.P. Morgan

Somewhat unrelatedly, but no doubt an essential tenet of those who put the quilt together, the first, or upper lefthand block, is embroidered, "Honor thy father and thy mother."

"We are proud to be Americans" is appliqued in the quilt's center with "The Townsend Plan" and patriotic symbols. This is the only applique on the quilt and the brilliant blue and red of this piece really stands out for this reason. The embroidery on the other blocks is done in red, yellow, and blue floss, primarily in outline stitches, with some satin stitching and daisy stitches.

Parallel lines of white quilting mark the blocks in the Townsend quilt. Eight-pointed stars done with double lines mark the corners of the blocks.

Townsend Recovery Plan Quilt.

Century of Progress Quilt.

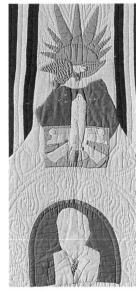

Century of Progress Quilt.

CENTURY OF PROGRESS QUILT

Applique and piecing with embroidery
By Mrs. W. B. Lathouse
Warren, Ohio, 1933
America Hurrah Antiques, NYC
82 inches by 66 inches

The *Century of Progress Quilt* was made in commemoration of the Century of Progress International Exhibition held in Chicago during the summers of 1933 and 1934. One of the greatest financial successes in the history of world's fairs, it was planned during a period of prosperity and successfully held at the height of the Great Depression. The exposition was designed to celebrate the one-hundredth anniversary of the founding of Chicago and to demonstrate a century's progress in many fields. Original plans were scaled down several times to meet the realities of shrinking budgets. The combined attendance during the two periods of the exposition was over 38 million. Foreign

participation was limited, as the plans for the fair were vague and confusing, but the modernistic architecture and colorful lighting had a lasting effect on industrial design.

Mrs. Lathouse, creator of the quilt, was a professional seamstress who came to the United States from Wales in 1922. She became a very patriotic citizen, celebrating the Century of Progress Exposition and United States history in this and in a victory quilt made in 1945. Both are ambitious tributes to America's strengths, history and leaders, with Mrs. Lathouse's quaint version of details framed in an arrangement with stars and stripes.

The quilt center features portraits of George

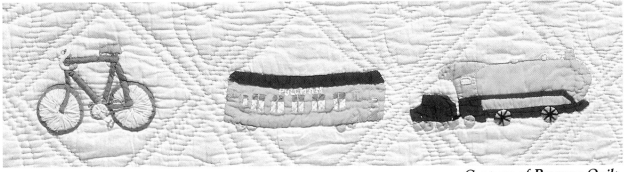

Century of Progress Quilt.

Washington, with "Father of Our Country" above and the hatchet and cherries below; and Abraham Lincoln, "The Emancipator," above a slave breaking from his chains. The unfinished bust of Roosevelt, who, elected during the Depression, was the "Hope of a Nation," gazes out over the Muscle Shoal Dam, a T.V.A. project, done in white-on-white quilting.

The days of long ago are represented in the lower center by the *Mayflower* with the Union Jack on its sail, a covered wagon and log cabin. Sunbonnet Sue was a popular figure in craft designs. Here she holds flowers appliqued from a fabric with floral designs.

In the upper section, between representations of the Stars and Stripes with the original 13 stars and with the 48 stars it had in the 1930s, is a glorious sun rising over an eagle with outspread wings predicting a great future for the country where the Washington Monument is a centerpiece of the Capitol Mall. Birds flutter in the blue sky about the white obelisk and pink flowers grace the areas between the walkways at the base.

In the quilt's corners are eight-pointed stars with the dates 1933 and 1833 stitched in gold. Across the top band are appliqued an airplane, touring car, and dirigible with a passenger compartment and the name emblazoned on the side. Evolution in transportation is represented on the right side by a streetcar, hot air balloon, tanker truck, Pullman car and two-wheeled bicycle. Across the bottom is the evolution of lighting: electric chandelier, kerosene or oil lamp, and a candle. Up the left side are all the important innovations in the life of the homemaker: the radio, telephone, icebox (with an open door which reveals among other food, a head of cabbage), vacuum cleaner, and washing machine of the wringer variety.

Solid blue scallops edge the quilt with the quilting done in concentric circles within each scallop. The white band features five-pointed stars; the red band is quilted with a representation of an eagle identical to the one which hovers over the Washington Monument at the center top. Squares and diamonds combine in the inner border with the appliques of progress in transportation and the household. In the center panel, the presidents are encircled with scrolled frames, and there is an assortment of anchors, crosses and horseshoes around them in addition to the use of contour quilting in the various scenarios.

Century of Progress Quilt.

Enrico Caruso Haberdashery Quilt.

Enrico Caruso Haberdashery Quilt.

ENRICO CARUSO HABERDASHERY QUILT

Log Cabin Straight Furrow in silks
Union City, New Jersey, c. 1920s
Laura Fisher/antique gifts & Americana
74 inches by 76 inches

This elegant *Enrico Caruso Haberdashery Quilt* version of the popular Log Cabin design known as Straight Furrow is composed of scraps left over from the haberdashery of the legendary Italian tenor Enrico Caruso. When Mrs. Da Silverstri of Union City, New Jersey, sold this quilt, she explained that it had been made by her mother and her aunt, who were employed by the prestigious Sulka Shirt Company of New York for thirty-nine years. Founded in 1895, Sulka was haberdasher to celebrities and the elite. Their specialty was making custom clothing from the most luxurious fabrics.

The two seamstresses took pride in their famous client at Sulka. They had worked on Caruso's haberdashery and saved scraps from the dressing gowns, pajamas, shirts and boxer shorts they made for the famed singer, whose voice during the early part of the 20th century made him the most highly paid and adulated singer in the world. Discovered in Milan, he debuted in 1903 at the Metropolitan Opera House in New York.

Caruso would have appreciated the mixture of elegant materials with the humble pattern of this quilt. Born in Naples, Italy, to the family of a

85

laborer, he learned to love the finer things in life. He loved good times, good food (a macaroni was named after him) and women. His love life was turbulant. A suit brought against him in court in New York, the Monkey House case, in which a young lady accused him of improper behavior towards her while viewing the monkeys at the Central Park Zoo, threatened his American reputation.

Renowned for his "coup de glotte," which became known as the Caruso Sob, a technique used to heighten the melodrama of his roles (critics sneered, but audiences cheered), Caruso last sang at the Met in a scene straight from an Italian opera libretto—singing "L'elisir d'Amore," the opera that led Arturo Toscannini to predict his amazing suc-

cess—he coughed blood on stage. He died in 1921.

The use of luxurious fabrics in quilts of the humble Log Cabin design became common in the 1870s. Many such quilts were displayed at fairs, paving the way for the advent of the crazy quilt, which replaced everyday fabrics traditionally used in quilt making with silks and velvets.

The mostly-pastel silk jacquard, a type of woven tone-on-tone fabric, is patterned with detailed Art Deco motifs—swans and snails, the Statue of Liberty and New York Harbor—and Jazz Age designs, such as cocktail glasses and champagne bottles. Even these scraps of fabric testify that the name Sulka was synonymous with the best, and appropriate for a quilted celebration of the Great Caruso.

LOG CABIN CRIB QUILT

Log Cabin pattern in cotton
Amish, c. 1920
Holmes County, Ohio
Esprit Collection
Photographed by Sharon Risendorph and Lynn Kellner

The *Log Cabin Crib Quilt* is constructed from sixteen Log Cabin blocks in bright and pale blue with the required red square at the center of each block. The manner in which these four quarters are assembled has created four saw-toothed diamonds, marked with red at the midpoint of their sides. As this is such a small quilt, not for a full-sized bed, only a single diamond of the background color, the deep blue, is created. The color choice of bright and pale blues with the traditional red center squares show that this quilter had an impressive command of color and an understanding of what she could do with her needlework skills.

The logs are quilted with stitches that follow the rectangular strips. This adds to creater durability in a quilt to be used on the bed of a child. The red squares are crossed with an X. Quilting in the pale blue frame is in pairs of oval leaf shapes, creating somewhat of a zigzag pattern. Stitching in a nicely executed cable fills the outer border of bright blue.

A crib quilt like this one with its brilliant color contrasts and geometric shapes must also be quite stimulating for the imagination of the young child.

Log Cabin Crib Quilt.

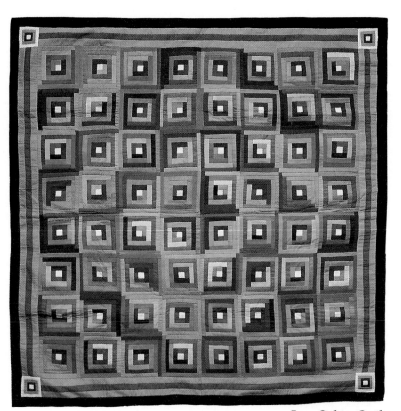

Log Cabin Quilt.

LOG CABIN QUILT

**Log cabin pattern in wools
Made By Sarah Kauffman
Lancaster County, Pennsylvania, c. 1861
Esprit Collection, San Francisco
Photographed by Sharon Risendorph and Lynn Kellner**

This *Log Cabin Quilt* is one of the earliest known Amish quilts. It was made early in the marriage of one Sarah Kauffman, whose husband was a fourth generation Mast of Gap, Pennsylvania. The Masts were known as "Church Amish" because they worshiped in a separate church building. Most Amish sects hold services in their homes.

The quilt is unusual for an Amish Log Cabin because the squares are built around a pink square rather than a red one. The quilt has a total of sixty-four blocks, and each block has only four increments of strips, which makes the intricate design of this quilt possible. The effect at first appearance seems to be one that takes considerable planning.

However, matching blocks strategically placed are not necessary to achieve this impression of alternating dark and light diamonds concentrically

arranged. The light side of each block is done in grays, purples, teals, light green or chartreuse, but in no special order. Sometimes the purple is in an outer "log" but it is often in an inner one. The dark side of each block is done in browns, teals, roses and rusts. When the dark sides and light sides are matched across the rows, such a composition as this results. A well-developed sense of the artistic in the quilter is important in the choice of colors used. Although the effect is achieved through random use of colored strips, the random choice occurs within a specific selection of limited choices and that is crucial.

By framing the diamond composition in bands of the pale colors, the quilter makes the background the pale colors. The diamonds in the deeper tones, including that at the center, stand out against the paler shades.

Diamond in a Square Quilt.

Diamond in a Square Quilt.

DIAMOND IN A SQUARE

Piecing
Lancaster County, Pennsylvania, 1925–1935
America Hurrah Antiques, NYC

Diamond in a Square is an Amish pieced quilt. No sampler of American quilts is complete without an example of the unique Amish quilts, a type which blossomed in Amish settlements in America from 1860 to 1940.

The Amish sect was started in 1693 in Switzerland when a Mennonite bishop, Jacob Amman, decided the Mennonites were not shunning worldly influences avidly enough (technology and higher education, for instance), and broke away to form what came to be called the Amish sect. After migrating to what is now Alsace-Lorraine, where they were harshly persecuted, they began leaving for the New World in 1727. Their first settlement was in Lancaster County, Pennsylvania, which remains the capital of the Amish world. Other settlements are in Ohio, Indiana, Illinois, Iowa and

Missouri. Today the Amish number 80,000.

The Amish people live according to strict rules. They believe simple living, hard work, self-sufficiency, humility and obedience to the Bible give meaning to their lives and hope for salvation after death. Among the many worldly influences forbidden them are photographs of themselves, which are considered prideful. For the same reason, children's dolls have no faces. Jewelry, even wedding rings, is forbidden, as well as automobiles, radios, private telephones and countless other conveniences most Americans wouldn't consider living without.

The Amish world is a world of blacks and grays. With almost all forms of the decorative impulse forbidden, homes are plainly furnished. But because it is functional, the quilt has always played a unique role in the lives of Amish women. It is their one chance to make something beautiful. They can escape the routines of their lives to gather together and finish a quilt. Thus, quilting is an important social and creative event for them.

The Amish used colors in a way that is startling and uninhibited. Cut off from the world of fashion and art history, they were not affected by styles and trends; they produced odd combinations of colors which distinguish their quilts from all other quilts. Surprisingly, religious restrictions regarding color in their dress did not seem to apply to quilts. Brilliant colors like magneta and even orange are combined with blacks and grays to produce unique effects. Early quilts are made from homespun wools, colored with natural dyes made from barks, berries, walnuts and weeds. Only solid colors were used. (Printed fabrics could be used in backings).

In Lancaster County, where this quilt was made, most quilts were fashioned in patterns of large geometric shapes: in some districts a quilt was considered a source of pride, and therefore unapproved, if its pattern was made up of many small pieces.

Because Amish patterns were nonrepresentational, there are no hints of personality or individuality, no suggestions of a favorite story, or an event being celebrated. Just as it was considered prideful to photograph a person—attempting to reproduce God's work—it would be prideful to set one's personal mark on the design of a quilt (although names of quilters are often embroidered at the quilt's edge). The quilting Amish women used to finish their work, however, belies the simplicity of their quilts' designs. It is as if the women, so restricted in their daily lives, were set free, their energies and artistic yearnings blossoming in designs executed twenty stitches to the inch. In the quilting they were allowed to reproduce earthly images. Feathers, wreaths, scrolls, roses, grapes, tulips, leaves and tendrils, baskets, hearts and stars are among the shapes ambitiously rendered.

Amish buggy.

At the center of this quilt is a star, symbol of fertility. It has eight points and many rows of quilting follow the parameters with a simple star in the center. It is surrounded with a feathered wreath. Rows of chain quilting fill the corners of the taupe square. The turquoise bands with four small taupe corners are quilted with a simple scrolling stem and five-petalled flowers. Ovate leaves branch off the stems and a flower is centered in each corner square.

The purple triangles around the center square have a three-cornered arrangement of stylized flowers with a long-stemmed rose-like bloom in the center, flanked by a pair of typically Pennsylvania tulip types, grouped with sprays of rose-like leaves. The quilting in the outer turquoise band is like that on the inner one, each side with six flowers. A pair of flowers face each other under each corner from which the scrolling vine with two additional flowers moves outward to the corner taupe square, centered by a flower.

The terra cotta band recaptures the chain pattern in the corners of the inner square. Here it is interpreted as an elaborate feathered garland that breaks in the center of each side as it meets the corner of the turquoise diamond in the inner square. While the outer bough of the garland terminates in a graceful curve, the inner one continues into a perfect loop in the taupe corner square, making a graceful composition before proceeding into the next side.

The reward for careful scrutinization of this seemingly simple Amish quilt is an exquisite aesthetic experience of color and geometric and curvilinear contrasts. There are actually three separate entities making a play of symmetry and balance: the intense colors, the geometric shapes, and the beautifully executed pattern in the stitching.

It might be said that this typical Amish quilt tells a collective story of womenfolk who lived by strict rules but for whom the quilt was a creative outlet. It was a means to flaunt their color sense which, restricted in their drab daily lives, could explode in glorious combinations. In collectively finishing off the quilt they could stitch earthly shapes lovingly, repetitively. Surely the functional purpose of their sewing was far exceeded in their quilt stitches. Their pursuit of beauty affirmed the bond connecting them with their more worldly sister quilt makers. Amish women didn't miss the pleasures of color and form, they just experienced them differently.

Bars Quilt.

BARS

Piecing in wools
Lancaster County, Pennsylvania, c. 1920
Esprit Collection
Photographed by Sharon Risendorph and Lynn Kellner

Bars is a distinct Lancaster County Amish quilt design. It, like other Amish quilts, has a central focus, typically set within one wide and one narrow border. Amish quilts are always worked in the solid color fabrics which the Amish wear under their somber-colored outer clothing.

Here the brightest and lightest color is used most sparingly—only the framework of the central composition is pink, and it is even broken at the corners. The deepest tone, the saturated turquoise, is also used sparingly in the corner framing blocks that anchor the composition and the outer edges. It is also the basic element in the central panel since the red is the common background of the entire quilt. The turquoise bands are the only element in the quilt which is not duplicated four

times: there are four corner blocks, four wide red border bands, four pink segments of the inner frame, and four small turquoise blocks. Within the framework are four red bars, but only three turquoise bars. When a person looks at the quilt, the three turquoise bars stand out in the pink frame, and the red background drops out.

In startling contrast to the basic geometric shapes and the simplicity of this design is the elaborate pattern in the quilting stitches, which tend to disappear into the background. First, in the wide outer red bands, the stitches outline lavish flowing plumes in curving S-shapes that fill the space. In the turquoise center block is a wreath of plumes, centered with a six-pointed star—finally a second element based on three.

Trouser Cuffs Strip Quilt.

Trouser Cuffs Strip Quilt.

TROUSER CUFFS STRIP QUILT

Pieced gaberdine
By Louella Powell
Bossier City, Louisiana, 1940s
Laura Fisher/antique gifts & Americana
66 inches by 80 inches

The *Trouser Cuffs Strip Quilt*, the epitome of the salvage art aspect of quilt making, celebrates better than any other quilt type the virtue of thrift upon which American society and quilt making were based. Thrift was a virtue crucial to the lives of the first Black Americans, who were inherently poor.

The first West African women brought to the New World carried with them a cultural memory of striped fabric and clothing which, since the 12th century, was constructed of strips woven on small looms. The strip quilt evolved from a combination of their native design with the three-layer Anglo-American quilt.

Where absolute repetition and symmetry are the hallmark of Anglo-American quilts, the strip quilt uses scrap material cut into strips, or strings, and sewed into an "offbeat" design that makes no attempt to match fabric patterns with seams. Bright colors, particularly red, considered a lucky color in Afro-American folk art, are always predominant. The lack of symmetry in strip quilts gives them an unpredictable, improvisational feeling: some students of African-American quilts have compared them to jazz, which uses improvisation and offbeats, rather than a musical score and a regular beat. *

This offbeat quality in strip quilts is too persistent to be attributed to the quilter's running out of a particular fabric and using whatever was at hand. Strip quilt makers have their own language to describe the way they plan their quilts: "I just cut 'em. Just as long as they look right, I'll fit 'em."** They don't speak of planning quilts: they talk about "building" them, "playing fabric."

Another feature of strip quilts that may seem to be a mistake is that they don't bother with straight lines. Strips curve, like snakes, another symbol of good fortune. Africans believed evil spirits followed straight lines. In her article on African-American quilts in *Clarion,* Maude Wahlman quotes from Judith Chase's *Southern Folklore Quarterly*** piece:

> Black slaves oftentimes refused to plow a straight furrow, or follow a straight line in a pattern without occasionally deviating to foil the 'malevolent spirits.

*"Who'd A Thought It?" Catalog from San Francisco Craft and Folk Art Museum Show, 1987.

**p. 28, Ibid.

Louella Powell was the granddaughter of slaves and made quilts until her death in 1970. Her quilt is assembled from the pants cuffs of work clothes; you can see the wear marks where the hems were let down. There is not a straight line in the quilt. It is built around a center focus according to the English format, which was always planned around a center motif. The center contains eight blocks which are diagonally pieced, with no effort to match patterns. It resembles a Log Cabin block except that where Log Cabin quilts are planned with precision to create visual symmetry, Mrs. Powell's quilt makes no attempt at such an impression. Her quilt's irregularity is quite intentional in the genre of strip quilts.

Since quilts made by African-Americans do not communicate any personal information about themselves, the unplanned, or improvisational quality of strip quilts prevents copying and preserves for each quilter her own unique design.

***pp. 47-8, "African American Quilts: Tracing the Aesthetic Principles," Maude Southwell Wahlman. *The Clarion,* America's Folk Art Magazine, Spring 1989, Vol. 14, No. 2.

PECOLIA WARNER'S " MAKE-UP QUILT"

Piecing, 20th Century
By Pecolia Warner
W.R. Ferris Collection, Department of Archives and Special Collections, University of Mississippi

Pecolia Warner.

Pecolia Warner, a black quilter born in 1901, learned to quilt in the traditional way girls learn to sew—from her mother. She called hours spent at her mother's side by the fire, watching her quilt, "fireplace training." "I been wanting to piece quilts ever since I saw my mother doing it," she said before her death in 1982.* "I wanted that to grow up in me—how to make quilts." She described how her mother would give her "little-bitty strings" of leftover material and how she would sew them together, then lay out the strips along the length of her bed and sew a plain strip between the pieces, making a string, or strip quilt. She recalled, too, her mother's quilting bees: as a child, she used to get under the quilt and watch the women's hands push the needles through.

When folk historian William Ferris* met Mrs. Warner he was struck by the sense of place suggested in her quilts as it is in so much Southern

Pecolia Warner's "P" Quilt.

folk art. "I was born in a log house. It was made out of logs with mud in between them and rough boards nailed on to hold the mud in there. And I've pieced up a log cabin quilt. It's a string quilt, and it's easy to piece."

She drew on her childhood memories also to make a pigpen quilt: "I dreamed one time about making a pigpen quilt, and I ain't never seen one made on a paper. I just remembered how we used to make pigpens for our hogs and I made it up. First you put a floor down. That'll be a solid piece, a square. And then you lay the rails all the way around the pen. See, you take a strip, that'll be your first rail, and you go all around the square. Then you get another strip of a different color, and keep going all the way around until you get the pen built. You don't skip it nowhere, you must keep coming all the way around. See, that's the frame of the pen. Then it'll be like a pen to put your hogs in. And that's just the way I made that pigpen quilt."

A popular symbol Pecolia Warner has used in her quilts is the pineapple, which she "built" into quilts as a variation of the star pattern. "My pineapple, that's pieced up like a star . . . see, but it's really a pineapple. I saw one in the grocery store—it wasn't peeled—and I just looked at it to see how it was made."

In her works and words, Mrs. Warner reveals herself and her life to others. She personalized this quilt with a "P" design she took pride in. She said*she was just " . . . sitting around one day and didn't have nothing else to do. So I said, 'I just believe I'll make me a piece that will be the start of my name.' I call it that "P" quilt. I just took me a piece of paper and drew the "P" with a pencil. You make it like if it was printed somewhere. Then you take your straight scissors and cut that "P" out. You got you a pattern, see."

Pecolia Warner considered quilt making her calling. Like Harriet Powers whose creations were the "darling offspring of my brain," she loved her quilts as a woman might love her children; like other women drawn to quilt making, she knew she was creating something of lasting value that would survive her. "I want people to keep them and remember me," she said. "They'll say, 'Well, I knew one old lady, that's all she did was to piece quilts.' I'd like them to remember me quilting."

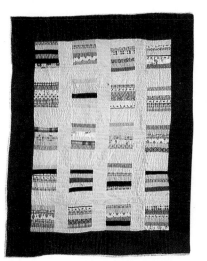

Pecolia Warner quilts.

Local Color: A Sense of Place in Folk Art, McGraw-Hill, 1982, and *Afro-American Folk Art and Crafts,* University Press of Mississippi, 1983.

95

Broadway Quilt.

Broadway Quilt.

STITCHING TOGETHER

In images of women making quilts in colonial America they sit alone in the flicker of firelight, or the dim glow of candles, working against the coming of winter at the end of a day's chores, proving the old adage that while men work within the boundaries of daylight, a woman's work is never done.

But quilt making, besides filling a physical need for warmth and comfort, also fulfills another important human need: the need for companionship and sociability. The quilting bee was an important event in the lives of 19th century women, as it is today in groups of enthusiasts who share a common cause and a love of quilting.

Except for the large cities on America's east coast—Boston, New York, Philadelphia and Charleston—America until recently was basically a rural society. The westward movement spread the population over vast areas, with settlers staking claims on isolated parcels of land. A rural character stamped American culture and customs until early in the 20th century. The quilting bee became the social event that perfectly matched the rugged pioneer spirit of America. Hence, the prized qualities of thrift and industry were present even during periods set aside for pleasure and company.

Mention is made in an 18th century book of a quilting bee that took place in 1752 and lasted ten days.* A hundred years later the quilting party was an established social event people traveled hours to attend, staying for varying amounts of time, bringing blocks of sewing they'd completed at home, completing numbers of quilts, celebrating, eating, dancing. Any household could hold a bee, since quilting frames were cheap enough for every household to own one. Poles and clamps could be arranged in a variety of ways to accommodate quilters, seated or standing. Set on the backs of chairs, or suspended from rings on the ceiling so it could be lowered for work and raised when not in use, the frame held the quilt fabric taut until the women had finished the areas they were working on. Then clamps were loosened, the quilt moved and new areas were ready to be quilted.

*p. 39, *Quilting in America.*

Meals were served, the less skilled steamstresses doing kitchen duty. Sometimes the men would come to eat, or for square dancing after the quilt was finished and the frame put away. Parties were held to finish an engagement quilt or a bridal quilt.

One custom among the many connected with quilt making was that after the quilt was finished, a cat would be placed in its center. "The unmarried girls and boys held edges of the quilt and tossed the cat in the air. The person closest to the spot where the cat landed would be the next married."**

Many quilting activities, including needlework lessons as well as bees, took place at churches, the center of 19th century social (as well as religious) activity. Women could gather there away from men, talk about their unique concerns—children, cooking, issues of particular interest to their sex. Quilting bees were, as the authors of *Hearts and Hands* illustrate convincingly, the earliest activity in American history where women regarded themselves as a group separate from men. Susan B.

**p. 53, Ibid. Since marriage was the only choice open to 19th century women dozens of customs and superstitions centered on it. Men, too, had to marry out of necessity if not for love, to gain a partner in the difficult work of running a farm or business, and to produce children as laborers.

Anthony is said to have made her first plea for equal rights with men at a church quilting bee in Cleveland, Ohio.

With their fingers flying, their tongues buzzing, their consciousness being raised, women used the quilting bee to address shared concerns—to raise money for a church, help a friend whose house and belongings had burned, draw attention to a national problem, such as slavery or alcohol consumption. Moral truths and professions of friendship were embroidered and written onto blocks, the history of a town or a church recorded in the design.

Today the tradition of making a quilt together to draw attention to a common concern, or draw together to mourn a shared grief, has been revived by women—and men—and expanded to address the deepest concerns of our times. Quilts speak an international language, and have brought together women whose nations are as important as their children's futures. Those who have worked together on a quilt are moved by the same soothing, therapeutic process that makes individual women devoted quilters. The shared experience, they say, is more satisfying than the finished product, for they feel bonding not only with the quilting tradition of the past, but with each other.

BROADWAY QUILT

Piecing, applique, embroidery, painted fabric, and other embellishments
By friends of the Broadway Theater
New York City, 1988
Courtesy Broadway Cares

The *Broadway Quilt* was made in 1988 by representatives from every area of the theater world to raise consciousness about AIDS and raise funds for AIDS care. As dazzling and showy as show business itself, the *Broadway Quilt* was the brainchild of John Butz, doorman at the Broadway Theatre, home of the long-running hit "Les Miserables." Butz, who is also an actor, is active in the group Broadway Cares, an alliance of producers, actors, union members, technicians and representatives of Broadway, off-Broadway and regional theaters which have joined together to draw attention to the AIDS crisis.

It was Butz's thought that a quilt would "stitch together" the theater community in a show of solidarity in an industry that has been badly hurt by the disease. The project was an instant success.

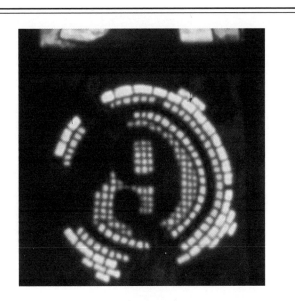

Details from the Broadway Quilt.

One hundred eight-inch square contributions came from backstage, onstage and all aspects of the theater. Applique, embroidery, needlepoint, beadwork and paint were used to produce the squares representing everyone from the ticketsellers to theater owners to the men and women who sew costumes.

Butz, who had never done more than sew on a button, made ten squares himself, including "1776," "South Pacific," "Sardi's" (famed restaurant where theater people gather to await reviews), and "Teahouse of the August Moon." Although he traced other designs onto fabric, this last one he drew on parchment and sewed over, then pulled away the parchment pattern. There are still a few traces of it on the "Teahouse" square.

The "Chorus Line" square uses as the ground the fabric used in the men's finale costumes. The logo is beaded and embroidered. Chita Rivera's dresser for "The Rink" did that show's square. Marion Elrod says she used basic embroidery stitches— zigzag, satin, counted cross. Details are drawn on in pencil. The square is autographed by Chita and by Liza Minnelli.

The "Les Miserables" square was passed around the cast and crew so that thirty-one members added at least a chain stitch to the logo-portrait, which copies the original woodcut used in show publicity.

Tom Morrow, creator of the poster for "Fiddler on the Roof," painted the show's square. Alyss Gilbert, wardrobe mistress of "M. Butterfly," appliqued the black satin block for that show, with her supervisor: he did the "M," she did the butterfly. (This is one of the few applique designs in the mostly embroidered quilt.) Alyss also coordinated the completion of the quilt. She had to convince John Butz that sashing and borders were necessary to separate the squares.

When the one hundred squares were completed, they were laid out on the stage at the Broadway so it could be determined how to arrange them. Consideration was given to balance between the dark and bright squares, for instance, but there were also diplomatic considerations. Two producers were not placed next to each other; current running hits couldn't go too close to the center "Broadway Cares" square, for fear there would be charges of favorites. When the squares were appropriately arranged, there was a quilting bee to sew them together and tuft the top to the bottom.

For those who worked on it, making the *Broadway Quilt* was a cathartic experience. It was raffled off for $25,000 at a celebration of Broadway Cares' first anniversary. The name of the celebration was The Quilt Show, with a program of actors performing numbers from shows represented on the quilt.

Civil War Quilt.

Civil War Quilt.

CIVIL WAR QUILT

**Piecing with ink inscriptions
Florence, Massachusetts, 1865
America Hurrah Antiques, NYC
88 inches by 52 inches**

This *Civil War Quilt* appears to be a group effort by many quilters—sisters, aunts, friends, perhaps—of a young man going off to fight in the Civil War. Its dimensions—it is unusually narrow—are not those of a conventional bed, but of an army cot. Since bedding was in short supply in hospitals and on battlefields, it is logical that women would have made a quilt for a soldier going off to war.

Friendship quilts were common in the 19th century when they were made by friends and given to someone undertaking a journey, particularly women going west with their families. They were usually scrapbag quilts, made from whatever each quilter had on hand, without any careful planning. Each quilter would make a square, on which she would embroider or write her name, and perhaps a poem or saying, as in the autograph books which were very popular at the time. Neither the design of the quilt, nor the quilting, usually just enough to hold it together, were important. The idea was to keep alive the memory of friendship, to have those memories keep the quilt's recipient company during the long years ahead.

This quilt was intended to keep alive in the soldier's mind the memory of people close to him, and what they stood for. Calico blocks were bound individually before the whole quilt was assembled and the brown calico border added. In the center of each block the quilters have written in ink sayings with a moral or patriotic tone, some of which bear comment:

Be true to humanity and to freedom.

Ye are martyrs to a good cause.

Northern women had supported the abolition of slavery since the 1930s. Through their needlework, which they sold at fairs, they were a major strength of the abolitionist cause.

Touch not intoxicating drinks.

101

Women's activism in abolition, plus their service to the male cause of war (providing supplies), no doubt armed them to invade male territory with their own war on the use of alcohol. In 1874 the Women's Christian Temperance Union, which would have far-reaching effects on America's drinking habits, was formed.

Other sayings in the quilt blocks include:

Quiet conscience gives quiet sleep.
Touch not tobacco—a curse on it.

Inscribed around the quilt's center is:

The Star Spangled Banner
long may it wave
O'er the land of the free
and the Home of the Brave!

Just above the flag in larger plain script is "Rally round the flag boys!" Also inscribed in a few of the blocks are decorations, such as the feather in the top left square and a scroll in the one beside it. On the left margin, one square up from the bottom, a wreath encircles the signature.

The quilting in each square is different, some squares having very little or crudely done quilting, as in the one with the pink corners in the bottom row. It is quilted in squares with very crooked lines. The blocks in the two top corners are quilted in parallel lines, but those on the right are much closer together. The left block in the second row is quilted more imaginatively. The white square is

Details from the Civil War Quilt.

The star-spangled banner
Long may it wave,
O'er the Land of the free,
And the Home of the brave!

Rally round the flag boys!

Flag of the free heart's hope & home, *wherever float that standard sheet*
By angel hands to valor given; *Where breathes the foe but falls before us,*
Thy stars have lit the welkin dome, *With Freedom's soil beneath our feet,*
And all thy hues were born in heaven. *And Freedom's banner streaming o'er us!*

Detail from the Civil War Quilt.

done with parallel lines on one diagonal, the red triangles on the other, and the background in parallel lines.

The two other squares with white backing are done in the same pattern: concentric squares with a diagonal cross in the center. Those with a pink ground on either side of the flag are done in an all-over pattern of concentric squares with a diagonal cross at the center.

This quilt shows no signs of wear and tear and it is therefore assumed that it was never used. Perhaps the young soldier didn't want to sleep under so many restrictions once he got away from home. It is possible, too, that he was one of the 600,000 men from the North and South who were killed in the war.

Boston Street Aid Society Quilt.

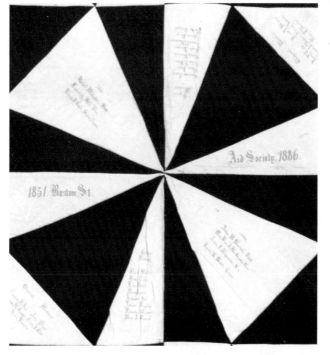

Boston Street
Aid Society
Quilt.

BOSTON STREET AID SOCIETY QUILT

Piecing and ink inscriptions
By Ladies of the Society
Lynn, Massachusetts, 1886
Lynn Historical Society, Lynn Massachusetts
Photographs courtesy Laura Fisher/antique quilts & Americana

The *Boston Street Aid Society Quilt* is evidence that religious faith was high in mid-century at Lynn, Massachusetts, and the four Methodist churches in town were bursting at the seams. When building a new church was discussed, James Pool, Jr., favored building in a poor section of town. He pledged $300—a large sum in those days—towards building on Park or Boston Streets; his choice for a site was agreed upon. The church was completed in 1853 in a spot which was believed to be a consecrated place. It was said that in 1813 an obscure youth entered the swampy land and threw himself to his knees. He had just heard a powerful sermon, and felt overwhelmed by his heavy burden of sin. He

prayed there until "like Jacob of old" he obtained the blessing.

Two years before the church was finished, the Ladies Aid Society was formed. Its first meeting, at the home of James Pool and his wife Clarissa, is documented by a patch near the center of the quilt, which was pieced and inscribed with ink information in 1886. The Society's meetings are described in a souvenir booklet published on the 51st anniversary of the church: a "small band of devoted Christian women—met regularly at one another's houses to bind shoes, finishing from 36 to 128 pairs at each meeting. A roll was called at each meeting, and those present were fined 6½¢."

Boston Street Aid Society Quilt.

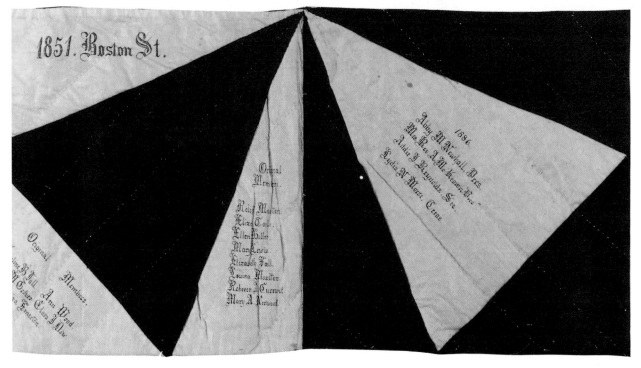

Boston Street Methodist Church.

At sundown on meeting days they partook of tea, which "by a fixed rule, consisted of milk-biscuit, cheese, one kind of cake, and tea." This rule was strictly adhered to. Once only was it broken. One good sister, at whose home the meeting was held, had been making pumpkin pies. Her husband slyly invited a few of the brethren into the kitchen and treated. As the first mouthful was taken, the ever-watchful secretary burst in upon them bringing the culprit before the officers. He was judged guilty and a fine of 25¢ imposed, which was duly paid to the treasurer.

Of great historical interest, the Boston Street church quilt is made up of red and white triangles arranged in the Winding Ways, or Wheels of Mystery pattern, a very old design not seen in 20th century quilts, and executed imperfectly here so that the optical illusion it creates is slightly "off." The red color, turkey red, was the most popular color used by quilters for over 100 years. A woman writing in *Woman's Magazine* praised its cheapness and its brightness, stating that it was a color "refreshing not just to the eye but 'through the eye to the inner sense.' "*

The causes for which the ladies made and bought provisions reveal how closely they were dedicated to not just the church itself (for which over the years they provided carpets, new pews, wall painting), but to pressing needs far away from Lynn, Massachusetts. Letters and records detail these good ladies' works. In 1855 they "made and sent a large box of clothing, valued at $50 to a mission in N. York City." In 1860 they sent objects, "suitable for a fair" to a clergyman in India, undoubtedly doing missionary work. Of greatest interest are the records of their many donations to Civil War soldiers. Both regular supplies and items for the sick and wounded are listed: comforters, pillows, sheets, quilts, medicines, cordials—these are inscribed on the quilt as well as entire letters from the U.S. Sanitary Commission, an organization that worked with the War Department to provide Union soldiers with supplies and medical care, thanking the women for their generosity to the Massachusetts Volunteer militia and "Our army before Richmond."

*p. 58, *Hearts and Hands*.

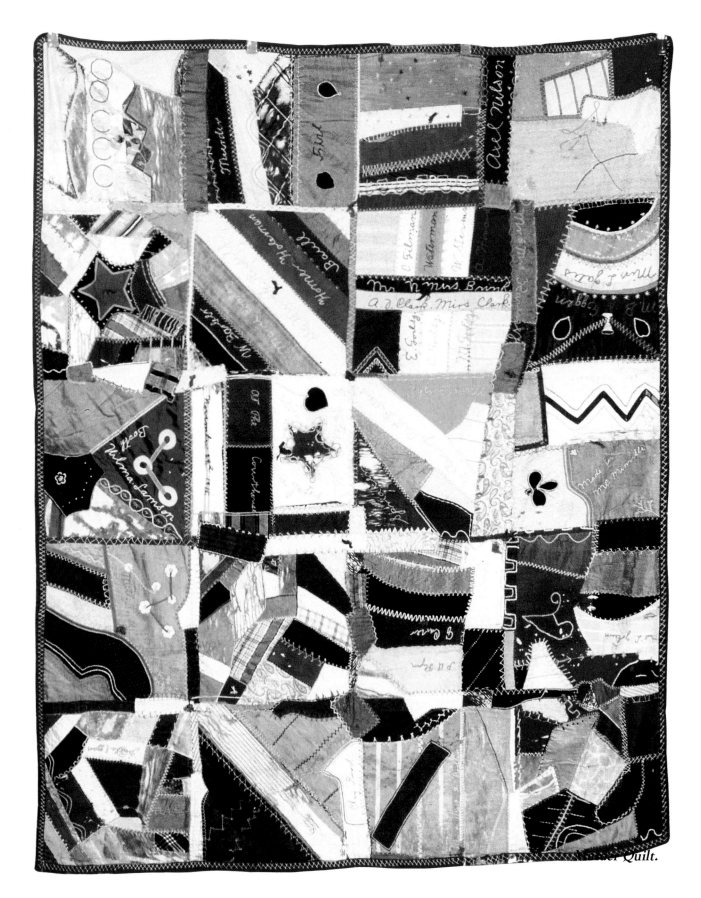

Quilt.

Murder Quilt.

MURDER QUILT

Crazy quilt of silk, velvet and ribbon, with embroidery
McMinnville, Oregon, 1915
Oregon Historical Society

The *Murder Quilt* is a one-of-a-kind friendship quilt, appropriately lugubrious in color, even with a few red velvet drops suggestive of blood. It was made and raffled off by residents of McCinnville, Oregon, in order to raise funds for the defense of two local residents charged with murder.

William Bramson and Anna Booth were charged with the murder of Mrs. Booth's husband William. Booth was found dead near a brick plant at Willamina on October 8, 1915, with a .38 caliber gunshot wound through the heart. The prosecution argued that he was killed after he had trailed his wife and Bramson to the thicket where his body was found. The case against Bramson and Mrs. Booth was largely circumstantial. It was reported that several months before the killing Mrs. Booth had threatened to kill her husband if he again accused her of infidelity. A farmer's wife who lived near the scene of the killing testified that she saw Mrs. Booth and Bramson "wending their way" towards the thicket ten minutes before she heard a gun go off. The coroner reported that Booth's wound was not self-inflicted.

Used as evidence against the defendants was a hair rat—a pad of hair used to add bulk to a hair style—the color of Mrs. Booth's found at the scene of the murder. A jury consisting of local farmers and a blacksmith found Bramson guilty of murder and sentenced him to life imprisonment. Mrs. Booth received a life sentence for second-degree murder. Their attorney requested a new trial.

A year later the case went to the Supreme Court. In March 1917 Bramson was again found guilty. A local paper reported that "young Bramson took the verdict with very poor grace, cursing generally and refusing to even kiss his mother." Mrs. Booth was sentenced to one to fifteen years in prison. At her sentencing the paper reported "the frail little woman" wept as she ended her remarks and marched out of the courtroom with Sheriff Sherwood. The newspaper account established the expense of the trial at about $2000.

Details from the Murder Quilt.

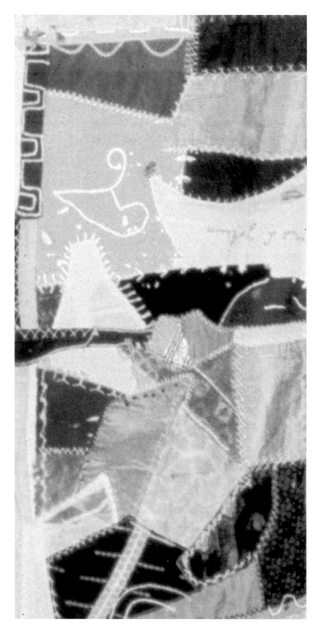

The *Murder Quilt* is embroidered with inscriptions such as "Booth/Wilma Lamson," "At the Courthouse," "November 29th, 1915" (the date the jury was assembled), "Murder Trial," "E. Gates/While/Waiting," "as witness," and "Made in McCinnville." Large yellow cross-stitching embellishes the quilt. A different name is on almost every piece, including that of Clay Rowell, who won the raffle and gave the quilt to his niece, who passed it on to the Oregon Historical Society. One of the rather curious patches is on the left where a goblet is appliqued between two red velvet patches above the names M. B. Eggen and Miss L. Gates.

WILLIAM BOOTH KILLED AT WILLAMINA
SUSPECT NOW IN THE COUNTY JAIL
AWAITING PRELIMINARY HEARING

Newspaper accounts of the Booth murder.

His Wife and Young Man Under Arrest Awaiting Action of the Grand Jury

Sheriff Henderson received word last Friday that a man had been found dead, shot through the heart, near the brick plant at Willamina. In company with Coroner Tilbury inquest was held all day Saturday over the body which proved to be that of William Booth, a local resident, aged 29 years, having a wife aged 30, a daughter 12 and a son seven.

The dead man is a nephew of Robert Booth, ex-County Commissioner, who was a foster father to William Booth for several years.

William Branson, aged 22, was first charged with the murder and placed under arrest and brought to the county jail on Saturday. The preliminary hearing of the case occurred on Wednesday, with R. L. Conner for the state and McCain, Vinton & Burdett for the defense. The entire day was occupied with the hearing. There were 18 witnesses called for the state and after their testimony was heard the defense waived further hearing. There were no eye witnesses to the shooting. The trial was before Justice N. L. Adkins who bound Branson over and Mrs. William Booth, arrested on the day of the trial, accused as an accomplice, to await action of the grand jury at its next term of circuit court which convenes November 8. Both accused persons are now prisoners in charge of the sheriff. The trial on Wednesday was held in the Willamina opera house, which was filled with interested citizens.

The fact that Mrs. Booth was seen in the vicinity of the crime so soon after it happened led the authorities to believe she might have known something which would clear up the case. Her arrest followed shortly after that of young Branson, who had been on bad terms with Mr. Booth for some time, the latter believing that Branson's attitude toward his family had been that of a homebreaker. Branson is the son of Mr. and Mrs. Arthur Branson of Willamina, and Mrs. Booth was a Harrington before she married, and resided in Happy Valley. It was revealed at the hearing that last August Mrs. Booth had threatened to kill her husband if he again accused her of infidelity.

Mrs. Mary Eggen, a farmer's wife, residing near the scene of the shooting, was the star witness. She testified that on the day the crime was committed she saw Mrs. Booth and young Branson wending their way along the road past her house near the brick plant, and shortly afterward she saw William Booth, the husband, following them. Ten minutes later she heard the report of the shot which killed Booth. A .38 revolver was used.

The verdict of the coroner's jury at the inquest was that the deceased came to his death from a gunshot wound inflicted by some unknown person, and not self-inflicted. The shot first took effect in the lower left arm, passing directly through the heart and lodging in the right side. The surroundings indicated that Booth might have been in the act of ——ing a fence. The gun that in——— wound has not been found. The ——ered man was buried at ———— Sunday.

THIRD JURY DECIDES
DEFENDANT IS GUILTY

William Branson Again Convicted of Murder in the Second Degree—Taken to the Penitentiary on Saturday

The third trial of Wm. Branson for the murder of Wm. Booth near Willamina on Oct. 8, 1915, came to a close last Friday, and the case was submitted to the jury about supper time. Before midnight they returned a verdict of guilty, and Sheriff Henderson the next day took the prisoner to Salem, accompanied by Henry Herring as guard. Young Branson took the verdict with very poor grace, as he did in the former instance, cursing generally and refusing to even kiss his mother.

Mrs. Booth, co-defendant, awaits her destiny at present in the county jail, and if no immediate trial is forthcoming, will probably be returned to the Multnomah county jail, until the regular sitting of the circuit court next May. The hearing of Branson's case occupied five days, and was quick work on the part of the court. The expense to the county is estimated to be about $2,000.

111

Hudson River Quilt.

Hudson River Quilt.

HUDSON RIVER QUILT

Applique and embroidery
Thirty women of Hudson River area
New York State, 1969 to 1972
Courtesy of Irene Preston Miller
96 inches by 79 inches

The *Hudson River Quilt* was part of a promotion to conserve the Hudson River Valley for posterity after Con Edison unveiled a plan in 1962 to construct a pump storage plant near a nuclear power plant at Buchanan, New York. Area residents were alarmed at the possible destruction of one of the Hudson's most beautiful landmarks, Storm King Mountain. Fishermen were also opposed to the project, which threatened the spawning grounds of the river's striped bass.

Irene Preston Miller owned a textile shop at Croton-on-Hudson where she taught classes and sold materials for all kinds of textile crafts. She had long been involved in conservation efforts, and,

combining her interests, conceived the idea of making a quilt to draw attention to the river's beauty and win support for its protection. The women Mrs. Miller brought together to design the thirty squares were not quilters; they were not chosen for their proficiency at any kind of sewing. They were women affiliated, one way or another, with the fifteen-year, eventually successful battle to preserve Storm King.

Among the women who worked on the quilt was Ricci Saunders, wife of the spokesman for Scenic Hudson; she made the Storm King square (first square, third row). The deep green mountain appears to rise out of the water where it towers over

Hudson River Quilt.

the sailboats. They are embroidered as is the tug pulling the barges at the left. So are the rails in the foreground. The piece is quilted to enhance the impression of waves on the blue water, and add more clouds to those that already billow in the sky.

Penny Cohen, sister of folksinger Pete Seeger, made the center square of the sloop *Clearwater*, coincidentally launched in 1972 when the quilt was first exhibited to the public. (It was the intention of Seeger to sail the sloop up and down the Hudson for educational purposes.) The serenity of the boat centered in the compass rose speaks to those who appreciate the waters for their nautical activities.

The thirty squares, connected by the red sashing, range geographically from the river's source at Lake Tear of the Clouds in the Adirondack Mountains (top left square). Water spills from the lake down the valley between the contours of the Adirondacks. The hillsides are in many shades of green with the quilting used to suggest mounds and rills, orchards and forests. Contour quilting surrounds the clouds.

Next to this in a combination of applique and embroidery is a delightful rendition of the Albany state capitol. The turrets are depicted in calico. In the distance are the meandering curves of the river. Embroidered fountains play in the reflecting pool in the foreground. In contrast are the squares in the bottom row of the Manhattan skyline and New York Harbor.

The composition in the bottom row of the red and white sailboat deserves special study. The white caps look like those in a Japanese painting, and the waves appear three-dimensional. A cloud scuds across the sky giving a real sense of movement as the boat is beating over the water before the wind.

Each woman's choice of subject matter and sewing style resulted in squares of varying moods. The scenes with the sailboats might well be described as lyrical, as might the excursion boat steaming through the palisades at the very top center. Note the effective use of the patterned fabrics on the rocky shoreline. There is considerable embroidery on the boat and the quilting stitches are used for wave detail and to simulate the ruggedness of the cliffs.

Hudson River Quilt.

Women quilting the Hudson River Quilt.

Some squares are historic—find Westpoint and Lyndhurst in Tarrytown (second and fourth squares in third row)—while others are nostalgic—the oyster shells and blueberry bushes in the second row, which symbolize a time before pollution killed off oyster beds and Indians who had migrated north returned for oyster festivals. Stitchery adds the details to this square and quilting adds more leaves to the blueberry bush.

A whimsical touch is in the last square of the fifth row. The sequined scales of the pink salmon glitter, while the back of the sturgeon looks like armor. The marvelous crest of the wave is accentuated by the spiraling quilting stitches. On the opposite border is a composition in praise of water birds—long-legged waders and swans included.

Tucked in as a favorite sight along the river at the time the quilt was made is "the violinist who practices by the river" (fourth row, above the fish), a figure frequently in view of those traveling by train above Yonkers. Here he entertains an embroidered seagull by playing with his arm over his head.

The *Hudson River Quilt* was begun in a decade when the interest in quilting, long in decline, had started to revive with the new interest in handcrafts of the '60s. At that time women were reconnecting with their inheritance of needlework. Shortly after this quilt was first exhibited in 1972 at the Museum of American Folk Art, a show at the Whitney Museum in New York is credited with elevating the quilt to the status of art.

Hudson River Quilt.

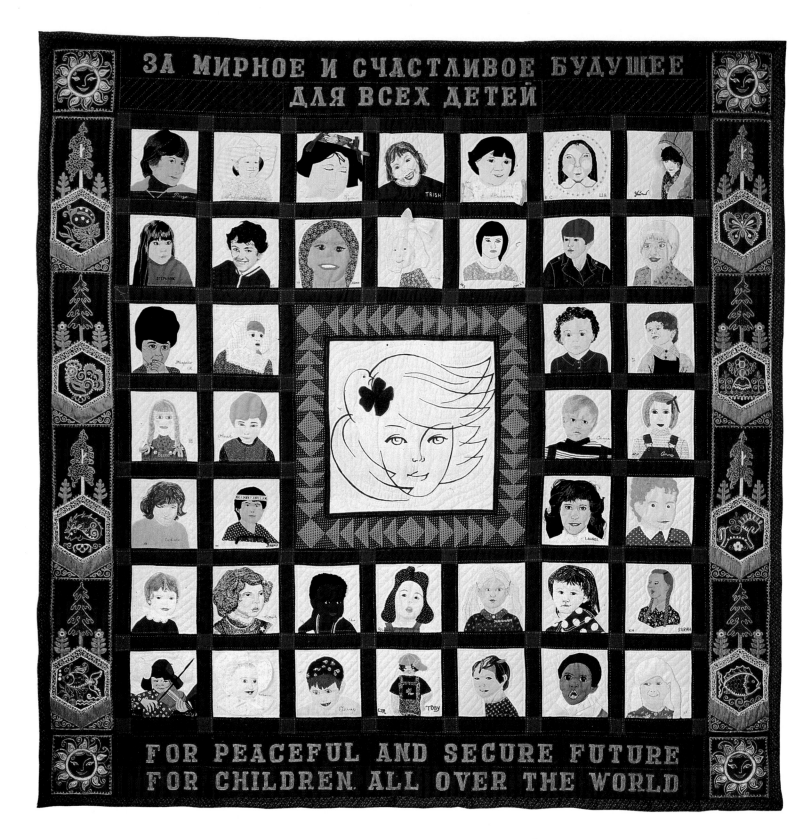

Soviet American Peace Quilt.

Soviet American Peace Quilt.

SOVIET AMERICAN PEACE QUILT

By American and Soviet women
1985
Courtesy Boise Peace Quilt Project

The *Soviet American Peace Quilt* is the work of the Boise Peace Quilt Project. Peace has always been an issue close to the hearts of women; while men have made the laws and declared the wars, women have felt a special calling to make the world a safe place for the generation they have borne and nurtured. With the burgeoning interest in quilts and quilting in the 1960s, it was only a matter of time before women would choose the quilt, pieced and sewed by women together, as a symbol of warmth and protection, as their way of participating in the world peace movement.

One morning in 1981, two women in Boise, Idaho, were discussing with horror the effects of fallout from nuclear testing in the 1950s in the nearby desert in Utah. They wondered what they could do to help keep the peace, to make sure the two superpowers would never conduct a nuclear war. Two things occurred to them. Believing that personal contact diffuses impersonal animosity, they wondered how they could make friends with ordinary Russians. The other thought came from the long tradition of using needle and thread to mobilize opinion by making a quilt. Thus the Boise Peace Quilt Project, a pre-glasnost people-to-people effort at peacemaking was born.

Ironically, neither of the women had ever quilted before. But their idea brought people who were uncomfortable about the usual ways of demonstrating for peace together to make quilts in the Boise

Peace Quilt Project and in more than twenty other quilting projects around the country.

The first Boise Peace quilt was made in 1981 and delivered to the Soviet embassy in Washington. From there it went on display in Moscow, eventually ending up in Lithuania, and resulted in correspondence and visits back and forth between the Boise women and women from the Soviet Union. In 1984 they decided to make a joint peace quilt. This quilt is the result of those efforts. Photographs of twenty American children and twenty Soviet children were collected; American women converted the portraits with needle and thread, paint and fabric, into quilt blocks. Women of the Soviet Union designed and worked the borders and the central figure, adapted from a Soviet peace poster combining a dove and girl's face.

In 1985 Heidi Read from Boise met with members of the Soviet group on the Isle of Wight to pin pieces of the quilt together. The finished product, which combines hand and machine applique, paint and embroidery, is stuffed with "peace fleece"—wool from both American and Soviet sheep. The Boise women then did the quilting. The quilt was hung in the conference room in Geneva where arms talks were held.

The center portrait adapted from a Soviet peace poster is painted. The few simple lines integrate the dove and the face. It is framed in red and then with a pieced border in red and yellow dots and a reverse of the pattern. The same shades are used in the embroidered border done so exquisitely by the Soviet women. The stitches are beautifully rendered with considerable skill evident.

NATIONAL PEACE QUILT

By Boise Peace Quilt Project
1984
Photographed by Mike Cordell

The *National Peace Quilt* is another quilt made by the women of Boise. It focuses on American lawmakers and contains a block designed by a child in each of the fifty states, with needlework done by the child's caretaker, not always a parent. Bordered with red and white stripes and with corners anchored by stars, it is reminiscent of the American flag.

Between 1984 and 1986, the *National Peace Quilt* was circulated among United States senators, who were asked to sleep one night under the quilt in hopes that they would dream of peace and wake to carry their dream into the world. Of the 100 senators targeted, 67 did sleep under the quilt. Those senators' names are embroidered next to the state they represent. The quilt then traveled around the country and will eventually hang in the Smithsonian in Washington.

National Peace Quilt.

SANTUARY QUILT

By Boise Peace Quilt Project
1988
Photographed by Stan Sinclair

The Sanctuary Quilt honors individual peace activists. It recognizes the struggle for freedom in Central America, where refugees continue to flee persecution in their homelands and seek sanctuary in North American churches.

The squares depict Central Americans who flee, some on foot, carrying all their possessions on their backs (the horizontal patch in the lower center). Under a nighttime sky, heavily laden figures of all ages are silhouetted against white buildings with tile roofs as a child urges them forward to a stucco church of typically Spanish design. The contours of the appliqued hillsides in the background are deep purple.

Above this is a striking panel in black and pink of an overcrowded truck, frightened people crammed in and dangling limbs over the side. Fearsome faces dominate the image as the vehicle plows through the darkness in search of sanctuary. Other striking images in the center of the quilt are the myriad of golden crosses on the calico field, the wide-eyed Indian family about to hatch from the egg with a church cross shining in the distant sky. Above that is a poster-like image of barbed wire across a masked face as the fingers of a brown hand reach over a barricade.

The killing and death, pain and sadness the refugees leave behind, as well as the beautiful landscapes of their native countries, are shown: in the middle of the left border friends and family gather around a casket strewn with flowers; church in the hills is the background. Below that is a crowd with placards begging for changes in the status quo—again a church is in the background.

In the blue panels across the bottom of the quilt is a summary of some of the events in the refugees' struggle for freedom. At right, a clutch of people are leaving with their few possessions for a journey toward the mountains; at left center, they are joined with a priest in front of the cross; at right center, a household welcomes them with open arms. The text beneath the figures states: "What does the Lord require of you? To act justly and to have mercy." At right is a colorfully striped awning above a welcome mat. The awning is scalloped below the words "REFUGEE RESETTLE-MENT CENTER." Here are smiling faces and potted plants.

The quilters made sure certain aspects of the sanctuary movement were included: squares honor specific religious communities and individual leaders of the movement, including one who raises goats. (In the center of the quilt on a turquoise background is a group of people with a white goat in the corner.) Next to that is depicted a person in prison—note the bars over the body—while in the background are two keeping a vigil with candles in their hands. Above that is a certificate of the Ann Arbor Public Schools, and a piece with the bearded man and group of ten memorializes several with names embroidered on the edges.

At the top there is a map of the United States, a dove and a helping hand. The Seattle waterfront—the city government has declared the city a sanctuary for refugees from Central America—is representative of all sanctuary cities. One of the most striking images is that below the outstretched hand with dove: a group of refugees is silhouetted as they stand on the rocky soil and stare into the brilliantly rising sun. A gray wall and ditch separates them from the bountiful trees in the distance, but the brilliance of the sun and its overpowering presence surely signifies hope.

Sanctuary Quilt.

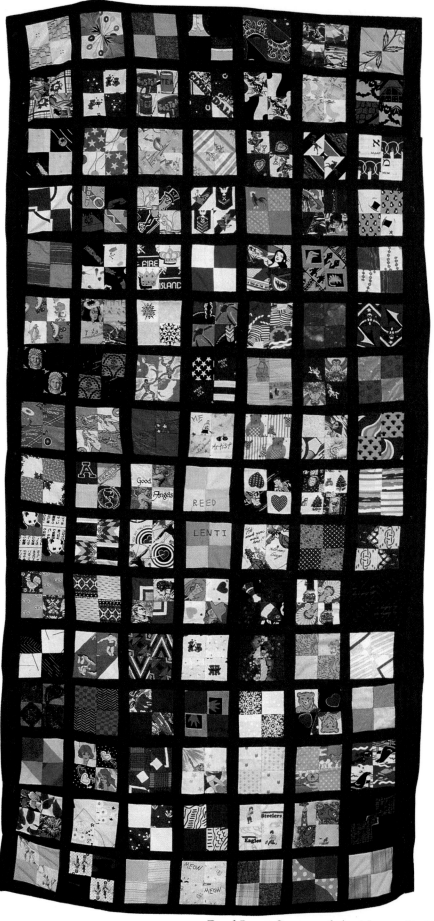

Reed Lenti Square of the Names Project AIDS Quilt.

Reed Lenti Square of the Names Project AIDS Quilt.

REED LENTI SQUARE OF THE NAMES PROJECT

Applique, piecing, embroidery
By Alan Isaksen

The *Reed Lenti Square* is a small part of the Names Project AIDS memorial quilt which is made up of thousands of panels, designed by people whose lives have been touched by AIDS. Each panel is a memorial to someone who has died of the disease. More than 9,000 people from 50 states and 16 foreign countries have contributed to the quilt. The Reed Lenti panel was made by Alan Isaksen.

Alan Isaksen placed Reed Lenti's name in the center of his quilt panel surrounded by squares made from fabric reminders of places they had been together and from scraps given to him by friends, as well as saved from clothing. Isaksen worked out a four-patch design, trying not to use the same fabric twice. Most of the quilt was put together by machine, except for the more fragile material, which was sewn by hand. The border and sashing is a corduroy-weave.

The Reed Lenti panel is one of several quilts made by Isaksen, who has long enjoyed quilt making. He uses fabrics he picks up on his travels and much that is donated by friends. To date he has made quilts only for his own pleasure, but in the future he hopes to sell some.

The quilt for Reed Lenti was started before Reed, an installer for a telephone company, died. Among

121

the fabrics that have special significance in this memorial are those with bears. "Reed was a bear," says Alan, "so I put bears in wherever I could." Next to the square with Reed's name is a four-patch with angels, and "Good Angel" printed on it. (Alan picked this up at an antique store where

he worked.) "Good Angel" was a song title. "He was a good person, so I know he's a good angel," says Alan. The cat fabric refers to the cats that the two kept, and the Planter's Peanuts squares came from clothing bought at a thrift shop in Atlantic City.

The Names Project

In 1987, a year after San Francisco resident Cleve Jones lost his closest friend to the AIDS virus, he came up with the idea of stitching together panels to make a quilt in memory of his friend and others who had died in a city that was particularly hard hit by the disease. His idea of turning something "hideous and ugly into something beautiful and powerful" eventually mushroomed into the memorial quilt. (In 1989 Guiness listed it as the world's largest quilt, although the panels are not joined, as in a conventional quilt.)

Every three by six foot panel in the quilt tells the story of a life and the loss felt by friends and family members who constructed the panels in order to work through their grief in a positive way. "Quilts represent coziness, humanity and warmth," says Jones, from the headquarters of the project in San Francisco's Castro District. One quilter heavily involved in the project put it, "To me the whole idea of quilting is to have a sense of community. The quilt represents the most beautiful way of bringing people together and of healing."

Describing the historical precedents for the Names Project, production manager Scott Lago points out that using fabric in the grieving process is as old as civilization itself. The Greeks tell of the three Fate: who spun the Thread of Life, measured it and cut it to determine the length of someone's life. A Jewish custom is for mourners to wear a torn article of clothing to symbolize that the "fabric of their lives" has been ripped apart by loss. "American quilting continues these traditions," Lago writes. "Quilts and the shared effort required to create them gave pioneer women a sense of community and a creative outlet to express many sentiments," about issues (abolition, temperance) and about friendship. Traveling west, the women relied on their quilts for emotional support. Sometimes a quilt was the only form of coffin used to bury the dead—thus, some women prepared quilted shrouds to say goodbye to loved ones.

Many elements common to the design of patchwork quilts have been incorporated in the AIDS quilt. The panels are assembled in nine-square units based on the popular Ninepatch design. The walkways between the panels, when the quilt is displayed, are arranged like the sashes which separate squares, in a conventional quilt. Many of the panels are signed with signatures or messages, as testimony of the friendship between survivors and those who have died, a tradition borrowed from friendship signature quilts.

The center of the quilt is a giant signature square where participants in the project and visitors to it can add a name or leave a message to someone they would like to remember. Done in rainbow colors, it is "a symbol of the promise of hope after a storm. I believe this rainbow epitomizes the purpose of this entire project," writes Scott Lago. "We can get through this horrible ordeal—and with this quilt helping to push the storm clouds out of the way. I think it's time to start looking for the rainbow."

Among the dozens of materials and objects, besides fabric, sewed into and onto the quilt panels are suede and lamé, blue jeans, a uniform jacket, stuffed animals, cremation ashes, locks of hair, beads, whimsy glitter, poems, letters, and a 100-year old-quilt.

Touring with the sixteen-ton project has drawn attention to the AIDS crisis, raised consciousness as well as funds to care for patients. In 1987 the quilt was displayed at the Capitol Mall in Washington, where it covered a space larger than two football fields. From there its national tour raised more than half a million dollars. The quilt is expected to increase in size as it tours, speaking for the suffering as well as stirring compassion for those affected by the controversial disease.

In November 1988 the United States declared a World AIDS Day. Panels of the quilt were unfurled from the balconies in the General Assembly foyer, where speakers reminded the audience that the quilt acknowledges the human face of the disease, that people do not die in masses, but as individuals.

In February of 1989 two California congresswomen nominated the Names Project for the Nobel Peace Prize. It isn't that the AIDS epidemic threatens peace between nationals, read their letter to the Nobel committee, but it threatens peace in society, which must struggle not only with the ravages of the disease but against fear and discrimination. "The AIDS quilt blankets the world of prejudice and fear with a sign of hope and sews a collective human face on this disease to heal the bitterness between people."

The AIDS Quilt on the Mall in Washington D.C.

A Representation of the Fair Ground near Russellville Quilt.

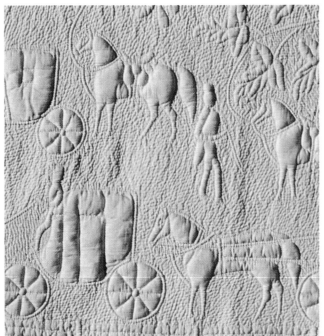

EMERGING FACES

With the immense interest during the past two decades in women's lives and their places in American history, quilts, often the only proof that women had, in fact, lived, have become important documents studied for clues to individual lives, trends, and customs. Prior to 1850, the existence of women was generally not noted in recordkeeping. In *Remember Me: Women and Their Friendship Quilts*, Linda Otto Lipsett writes that "only the names of 'heads of family' were listed in government census records . . . a woman's name was listed on the census only if she herself were the head of the household due to the death of her husband."* Further, records that were kept were often lost, or there may have been no records. New York State, for example, did not record births and deaths until 1880. The detailed genealogies, family histories and town histories, which were fashionable, rarely mention a man's wife. Only the quilts, made in profusion, especially between the years 1800 and 1880, survive to bear witness to the lives of pre-suffrage and pioneer women.

Quilts were often signed and dated with cross-stitching or ink. The earliest signed quilt is presumed to have been made as early as 1793. Initials and names were sometimes appliqued, as in the *Folk Farm Quilt*; sometimes human hair was used to cross-stitch initials. Friendship quilts, made in great numbers during the periods of migration westward, were a daily project for many women, whose names appear sometimes on several quilts that have survived. A scrap of a woman's dress sewn into a quilt block, though, is as close a look at the woman behind the name as a quilt is apt to contain.

Except for those in urban areas, who might sit for a family portrait, or country dwellers, who might hire an itinerant painter to capture a family's image, few portraits of early Americans in the pre-photography era survive. Some rare diaries and journals record personal thoughts of the woman who kept them, although entries are more apt to be laden with adages and moral wisdom.

Quilts, then, were more a record of a woman's virtues and tastes than her personal life, her diligence, endurance and patience more than any thoughts unique to her. Amish quilters were actively forbidden to impose on their work any hint of their personalities—freely-designed applique designs, for instance—as being too prideful, too worldly, and an affront to God. Along with the deep faith that sustained pre-20th century American women through life's hardships was an acceptance of their fixed roles as silent servants whose reward would come eventually in heaven.

It is a part of the fascination with old quilts that they are accompanied by the shadowy figure who bent over them for hours, sewing pieces together as her mind pursued its independent life. In her book on quilting, Marguerite Ickis reported the thoughts of one great-grandmother quilter that were passed on to her:

It took me more than twenty years, nearly twenty-five, I reckon (to make her quilt), in the evenings after supper when the children were all put to bed. My whole life is in that quilt. All my joys and sorrows are stitched into those little pieces. When I was proud of the boys and when I was downright provoked and angry with them. When the girls annoyed me or when they gave me a warm feeling around my heart. And John too. He was stitched into that quilt and all the thirty years we were married. Sometimes I loved him and sometimes I sat there hating him as I pieced the patches together. So they are all

in that quilt, my hopes and fears, my joys and sorrows, my loves and hates. I tremble sometimes when I remember what that quilt knows about me."**

The quilt contains the quilter's secrets but cannot reveal them to the rest of us, or help us picture, except in a general way, the quilter and her milieu. Some quilts, though, do survive with clues to the quilter's individuality, life style, intentions. A daguerreotype (an early type of photograph invented in 1837), names, professional and geographic data, the quilter's style—these and other bits of surviving history can be read like tea leaves. Although most quilters and their life stories are lost in the mists of history, it is sometimes possible to piece together a chapter, at least, in the story of the quilter and her work.

*p. 29, *Remember Me: Women and Their Friendship Quilts*, Linda Otto Lipsett, The Quilt Digest Press, 1985.

**p. 270, *The Standard Book of Quilt Making and Collecting*. Marguerite Ickis, Dover Publications, Inc., 1949.

REPRESENTATION OF THE FAIR GROUND NEAR RUSSELLVILLE, KENTUCKY

Stuffed whitework
By Virginia Mason Ivey
Kentucky, 1856
Smithsonian Institution
86 inches by 89 inches with 4 ½inch fringe

Virginia Mason Ivey.

This *Representation of the Fair Ground near Russellville* is one of the 19th century's most important surviving quilts. It is no coincidence that it came from Kentucky, which, far away from the European-dominated original colonies, developed rich and varied styles unique to the region.

Virginia Ivey was born in Tennessee in 1828, named for her father's native state, and lived most of her life near Russellville in Logan County. She had no formal art training but had an innate understanding of perspective and a creative instinct that make her two surviving quilts, this one and one at the J.B. Speed Art Museum in Louisville, masterpieces of the art of quilting. Wherever she went she took her quilts with her, exhibiting them at fairs like the one she pictures here and winning prizes with them. After her father died she lived

Detail from the Fair Ground Quilt.

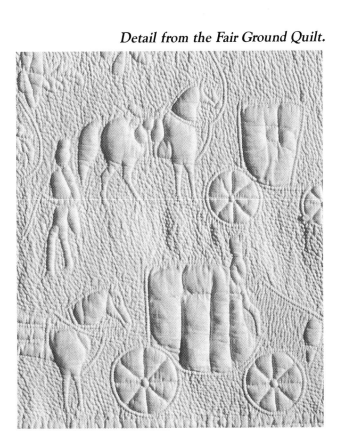

with her brothers in New Orleans and Illinois. She never married, a fact that perhaps explains the magnificent perfection of her painstakingly worked quilts.

In whitework, white fabric is quilted with white thread to create a design. White quilts were popular from the end of the 18th century to the middle of the 19th century. The stuffed work and stippled quilting (stitches pulled slightly to make fabric pucker) enhance the sculptural quality of Miss Ivey's work. Cording (the introduction of a cord onto the surface of the quilt through a channel prepared for it) is used in the vines.

In her celebration of the fair at Russellville, Miss Ivey uses needle and thread to record every detail of the event and suggest liveliness and motion in renditions of men and animals that are amazingly realistic.

The center circle is edged by a board fence with every board delineated. Immediately inside the fence in rather large letters is quilted "1856 A REPRESENTATION OF THE FAIR GROUND NEAR RUSSELLVILLE, KENTUCKY." In the circle's center is the judges' pavillion, with a ladder leaning against one side. Two men on the upper floor and four men below wear tail coats and tall

hats—on the upper level on each side of the center post; on the lower level each stands in one of the recesses behind the supporting posts. Pack and saddle horses and grooms, horses pulling surreys, horses with riders, cattle, roosters and hens, and sheep circle the pavillion.

On both sides of the judging circle men are visible in the doorways of lattice-work buildings. Four stately trees with elegantly feathered branches mark the four corners of the grounds. Clusters of nuts bough down the limbs and vines twine around the trunks. Between them along the edge of the quilt are smaller trees of a different species, one on the left with birds in its branches. Men walk under the trees, shaking hands, talking, riding horses or driving carriages; horses are saddled, or pulling surreys and carriages. Some of the men carry walking sticks or riding crops; there is a dog near the upper left corner. A board fence with gates runs around the quilt's outer edge.

It is estimated that the Russellville Fair Quilt contains more than 1,200,600 stitches. That is highly possible considering the extensive detail. In her portrait, Miss Ivey appears to be a woman of determination and stability, someone capable of such an ambitious creative work as this quilt.

Bird of Paradise Quilt.

Bird of Paradise Quilt.

BIRD OF PARADISE

Applique on muslin
Albany, New York, 1858–1863
Museum of American Folk Art
Gift of the Trustees of the Museum of American Folk Art
84 inches by 69 inches

This *Bird of Paradise* bridal quilt, named for the bird near the center with the sweeping multi-colored tail, has one particular feature that has provoked widespread speculation about the story behind the quilt.

Traditionally, the bridal quilt was made by a young woman after her wedding date was set following an old English custom popular in the colonies. A girl began making quilts when she was very young, generally finishing her first one by the time she was seven. She made a dozen quilts for her wedding chest, enough to cover all the beds in her house until she had daughters old enough to make quilts. The thirteenth, or bridal quilt, was started only after she and her family had chosen a husband for her. The bride then entered marriage with a baker's dozen of quilts.

The bridal quilt, since it was to be used on the couple's marriage bed, was the most elaborate of the quilts. Many superstitions were associated with it. One was that it was bad luck for the bride herself to stitch, draw, or even accidentally touch any hearts incorporated in the quilt's design. In fact, even including hearts was considered by some to bring bad luck. Others believed the bride shouldn't do any work at all on the quilt herself.

This quilt, made of wool, silk and velvet appliqued on muslin, is crowded with flowers, animals and all kinds of birds. The mysterious feature of the quilt is the space next to the figure of the girl where a male figure might be expected to appear. Instead, this space is filled with leaves and flowers.

When the quilt was discovered, with it were some of the templates pictured here which were

Bird of Paradise Quilt template.

used in the quilt's design. Templates are patterns—these are made of newspaper, cardboard and wrapping paper. Visible on one is an ad for Mrapps Book Bindery and on the bird is part of an 1862 almanac advertisement. The patterns are traced onto the fabric, then cut out a little larger than the traced shape to leave fabric to turn under before the shape is appliqued to the quilt backing, in this case, the muslin. With this quilt was found a template for both a male and female figure. The female template was used but the male was obviously not.

Since the quilt is unfinished—only the top exists—it is assumed something happened to the groom. The quilt was made during the period of the Civil War, making it very possible that the groom went off to war and never returned. Worked into the design are many hearts—on the lower left, appearing like apples on a bough, and on the tunic of the elephant keeper. Perhaps the bride had too much to do with making the quilt and her marriage was doomed by her committing some of the acts the superstitious womenfolk believed would sabotage it.

The young woman on the quilt strikes the identical pose of the template. In her one outstretched hand she offers a beautifully appliqued bunch of cherries, all out of proportion to her body, but

evidencing familiarity with the way cherries grow. She has a dark red bodice, bouffant blue sleeves, and petticoats under her pink skirt. Her hair-do bears a striking resemblance to that of the woman in the daguerotype sold with the quilt at the time of purchase. In composition with the gently curved foliage that fills the remainder of the square, she completes a circular composition, demonstrating the artistic good sense of the needlewoman who created this quilt. Proceeding clockwise around the quilt is a square with vining grapes being approached by a brown bird, resembling a thrush, in full-winged flight. Below that is an artistic arrangement of strawberries, grapes, apples, pears and cherries with their complementary leaves. Two stylized floral arrangements follow before the corner composition of a nondescript red bird perched among undefinable red buds and leaves.

Moving across the lower squares is a pair of red-winged blackbirds with a nest among branches and an elaborate composition centered by an urn towering with pale fruit. Four moths, one done in white and gray at the lower right, apples and birds resembling scarlet tanagers fill the space. In the left corner is a robin with four eggs in a nest in an oak tree.

Moving up the left side blocks of the quilt is a more exotic bird, a peacock, with a somewhat spread tail and a golden crown of feathers, in repose beneath a spray of flowers. Above that is a delightful square with strawberry plants, and then in sharp

Bird of Paradise Quilt template.

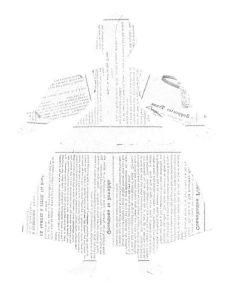

Daguerreotype of quilter.

contrast two vultures, hidden except for their weighty talons, among hickory leaflets. At the top is a stylized topiary with bell-shaped flowers that two hummingbirds find irresistible.

The six panels in the center include a menagerie of interesting creatures. The single square without wildlife is an exquisitely shaped urn on a fringed and scalloped cloth over a table exhibiting precisely turned legs. The fabric used for the urn is patterned, so the urn appears to have repousse. A red and a green apple, both the epitomy of perfection, rest on either side of the urn.

Next to this is a square with two peacocks, less realistically rendered than that on the lower left side. In the square with the birds is a magnificent moth with considerable embroidery in pale golds. Finally at the right center of the quilt, sitting in an oak tree, is the bird of paradise, the source of the name of this quilt. No attempt has been made to duplicate the realistic appearance of this bird in nature. Under the lower left oak leaves is a paper ticket that names the bird.

The pair of ostriches, on the other hand, are realistically colored. Below them are two panels containing several animals. With another beautiful pale moth, that seems to balance the one above, is what appears to be a black and white guinea hen, a rooster, cat, heavy black dog and then scenes from a circus: two elegant horses, named Ivory Black and Black Hawk, standing proudly over a water barrel. Below them is Hanibal the elephant, with rope secure around his tusk and in the hands of his trainer. The costume of the trainer merits study: he has epaulets, a studded belt, and a heart on his chest Bands around his wrists match his belt, and his trousers are red and brown, most likely to indicate that they were partially leather.

Whenever the creator of this quilt saw this animal trainer, she took in all the minute details of his apparel.

Returning to the top of the coverlet and the outermost border, a graceful garland of red and white calico buds bloom, all with yellow centers except for the one in the exact corner. The garland does not continue down the right side to balance the composition as one might expect with such carefully executed applique. Alternating red and yellow apples continue the border, ending with two red apples that dwarf the hawk-like birds perched on them—some kind of raptor because the legs and talons are so heavy. In the center of the right border is a pair of magnificent black horses, labeled "Flying Cloud" and "Eclipse." Their miniature, riders astride identical blankets, are doll-like by comparison, but they have gold pant stripes and gold details on their collars and at their waists. Two pale vultures sit on oak branches above an elegant moth. There is a silhouette of a hawk and then a pair of owls, one is calico, the other white and disappears into the background. The pair face another calico owl—all three sit on spindly arching oak twigs over black and white patterned birds that may be starlings.

In the bottom center is another pair of black horses facing each other, these with riders in better proportion. The riders are identical to those on the right side; these horses do not have names. There follows a leaf motif cut from one of the templates—this is the least delicate of all appliques on the quilt. Two beautifully cut red-winged black birds sit on nicely executed oak branches, then there is a robin and a red-winged blackbird in flight, finally two immense black-labrador-type dogs being ridden by another pair of doll-size men.

Story Quilt.

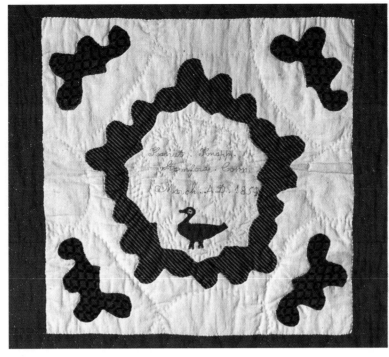

Story Quilt.

STORY QUILT

Applique
By Harriet Knapp
Stamford, Connecticut, 1854
Stamford Historical Society
100 inches by 87 inches

The *Story Quilt* has been inscribed with the name Harriet Knapp in the green wreath with the duck just to left of center. It also includes her place of residence and the year the quilt was finished. She was noted for her fine stitching but not much else is known about her. Her application of the twining floral vine in the border of the quilt is a demonstration of very careful work in cutting, stitching and applique. The maple leaves and stylized red buds alternate with pairs of facing leaves. The maple leaves are especially delicate. The design of the template used, to begin with, was an accurate depiction of the leaf, suggesting that a real leaf was used as the original pattern. Each projection is carefully defined with smooth neat edges. It must have taken incredible patience and long hours to turn the edges under so evenly. No fraying or loose threads are visible. The pairs of leaflets are equally delicate, but very simple. By comparison the red buds are somewhat crude because of their large size. They are well cut and all have smooth edges.

Two fabrics are used in the border. A very fine stripe in black and yellow green is used for the vine and leaves. The vine is cut on the bias as are most of the leaflets and maple leaves. The base of the red buds is cut with the straight of the goods, a small design element that one sees when examining the details. The red of the buds is the same fabric as that used between the blocks, a good choice that works to unify the elements of the design.

The blocks in the quilt contain objects used in daily life at the time the quilt was made—a can-

133

dlesnuff, a two-tined fork, scissors, a key, yokes for oxen, as well as farm animals and decorative items such as hearts and leaves. The green and red flower-and-vine border provides a cheerful frame because the colors of the calicos and fabrics the needle-woman used are as bright today as they were when the quilt was made more than 100 years ago.

The childlike simplicity of the animals and other figures the quilter has included, as well as her choice of subject matter, suggest that Harriet Knapp was a school teacher who used her quilt as a teaching aide to instruct her pupils in a unique way about familiar objects in their environment.

If she was a school teacher, it is also very possible that the individual blocks are based on the work of her students. This seems a likely possibility when one looks at the individual renditions of the animals. The two silhouettes of the horse are fairly sophisticated. But there are six cows, some of which are so crude that it seems impossible they were done by the same person who did the horses or the two representations of bulls in the center row with the wreath. The representations of birds also show varying degrees of maturity or skill, the rooster and hen in the next to bottom row being somewhat sophisticated. The arrangement of decorations around the perimeters of each block is rather childish. Most blocks are composed of a single fabric which further suggests each may represent a single student. The colors of the fabrics are all dark and rather intense, except for the two pastel squares, the one with the hearts and the one with the pink bird.

The quilting follows three patterns. In the quilt blocks it is done in large scallops around the decorative elements; in the red bands, it is done in parallel zigzags. And in the outer border it is far more ambitious, adding leaflets and blooms to the vine, as well as other floral motifs along the narrow red binding.

Story Quilt.

Blackboard Quilt.

BLACKBOARD QUILT

Embroidery on wool
By Nettie Ruby
Pennsylvania, 1906
America Hurrah Antiques, NYC
82 inches by 72 inches

The *Blackboard Quilt* was made in the first decade of the 20th century. By the turn of the century innovation in quilt design in America had ebbed. Few applique quilts survive from this period. Everyday patchwork quilts continued to be made, mostly in rural areas as more sophisticated city folk and even rural women were making crazy quilts, the dominant quilt style for those who wanted to show off their needlework and creativity.

This one-of-a-kind quilt uses a simple outline stitch on black wool as chalk might be used on a blackboard. Its design includes simple geometric shapes and drawings, and simple spelling words—doll, see, me—scattered with little apparent planning on the ground fabric. The quilter is presumed to be Nettie Ruby of Chapman Run, Bedford County, Pennsylvania, who is thought to have made it for Martha E. Miller upon her retirement, or when she moved away. Lacking any quilting techniques whatsoever, this quilt could just as well

have been a blackboard and chalk design.

The designs in the quilt are reminiscent of those made when one is doodling. The concentric circles and three-dimensional boxes especially call this to mind. It is also a sampler of stitches, especially the panel right of center; it contains feather, cross and herring bone stitches; the simple outline stitch is used elsewhere.

Since this is a quilt, or bed covering, one has to relate the pattern here to those used on quilts. The diagonal lines, floral shapes, hearts, stars, concentric circles, and medallions are certainly patterns used for quilting. The two renditions of houses are of the type appliqued on ambitious quilts of the 19th century. Finally, the six panels to the left of center are a careful rendition in embroidery of a popular eight-pointed star pattern used in quilting and patching. This may be an expression of appreciation for the art of quilting, or even a teaching aid.

Iowa Farm Quilt.

Iowa Farm Quilt.

IOWA FARM QUILT

Applique
By Marianna Hoffmeister
Hennepin County Historical Society
1880

Marianna Hoffmeister's picture of her farm in *Iowa Farm Quilt* is startling. Historical records indicate that she was born in Germany in 1827 and married the Reverend Hoffmeister in New Orleans in 1848. The palm trees and vaguely surreal flower shapes near the house in this fanciful rendition of her farm may be from memories of the time she spent in semi-tropical New Orleans prior to experiencing the more restraining life of a farm in Iowa.

A farm represents order. The challenge of those who work a farm is to control nature, bring order to it by planning out rows and acres, work with the seasons to produce crops. Mrs. Hoffmeister has certainly given order to her farm—a new one. An impression of joy, fantasy, and bold surprise dominates the composition which includes palm trees, a Disney-like representation of animals, brilliant lights in a dark blue sky, all constrained within a neat border of appliqued flowers.

The Hoffmeister quilt gives a first impression of a dark composition within a brilliant light frame. In fact, the framing fabric equals more than half the area of the quilt, but if one considers the appearance of this quilt on a bed, the farm scene would be paramount. The stylized blooms of the outer border are indeed attractive, with the serrated edges of the leaves and carefully executed and appliqued flower heads. Colors are nicely coordinated and subtle. Concentric bands of tan form an effective transition to the central composition.

The intense shades of the center panel are stark, and somewhat a surprise and refreshing change from the prettier colors customarily found in most decorative stitchery. One of the first details that the eye notices is the stars and the night-time sky. The swirling concentric stitching of the quilting reminds a viewer of the night skies of the artist VanGogh. Whatever the inspiration, the rendition

137

Iowa Farm Quilt.

of the sky is certainly a startling one to find in rural Iowa during the 19th century.

If that does not amaze, the tropical moon shining through the palm trees will. One wonders why the quilter chose the predominating brown materials for the composition. They make the farm look dry rather than fertile and productive. (One hundred years is a long time for fabrics to maintain their true color; originally they may well have been different.) The flamboyant hollyhocks by the dooryard give the opposite impression. They are outlandishly large and profuse in their bloom right next to the house.

Horizontal rows of quilting delineate the siding of the house, which appears to be a bright and airy living space with its tall windows, and a pleasant one with its bright centrally placed door. The huge white-chested dog standing on its rear legs under the palm tree appears to be a friendly beast who wishes he could get in on the action taking place down in the farmyard beyond the tree row and rail fence.

The four trees in the mid-ground are not easily distinguishable in their brown tones against the brown meadow. This area is quilted in concentric circles. A pale stream shimmers blue as it passes through the meadow on the way to the farmyard. Along it grow immense bell-shaped flowers, probably inspired by meadow flowers with which Mrs. Hoffmeister was familiar. The dark rail fence cuts a slice right across the compostion, separating the house and meadow from the farmyard and the action of the scene.

Even though there is a brilliant moon in the night-time sky, a younger member of the family is playing with a boat in the stream across the water

Iowa Farm Quilt.

from the parents. If this is a real farm family, it is unusual that there is only one child—there should be a whole flock of them—especially on such a farm as this . . . palm trees, etc. The woman, attired in long dress and apron, seems to be shooing some of the animals along in front of her: sheep, ducks and a big cow—all of a size that would surely be a physical threat to humans of such small comparative stature. The man of the family, with gun in hand, proceeds towards an outbuilding where an owl sits boldly on the roof. The owl seems to be the object of everyone's attention, except for the child, and is living proof that this is truly a night-time scene.

The multitude of the whimsical details on this Iowa farm indicate that the quilter was a person of vivid imagination who really enjoyed her days on the farm. The portrait of Marianna Hoffmeister from the Hennepin County Historical Society depicts an older woman who appears rather stern. The dates for her lifetime are 1827 to 1910. She did indeed live a long life for a woman in rural Iowa in the last century. We know that she was age 21 when she married and age 53 when she made this quilt. She and her minister husband had years of hard work behind them at the time she completed her whimsical representation of their homestead.

Marianna Hoffmeister.

Iowa Farm Quilt.

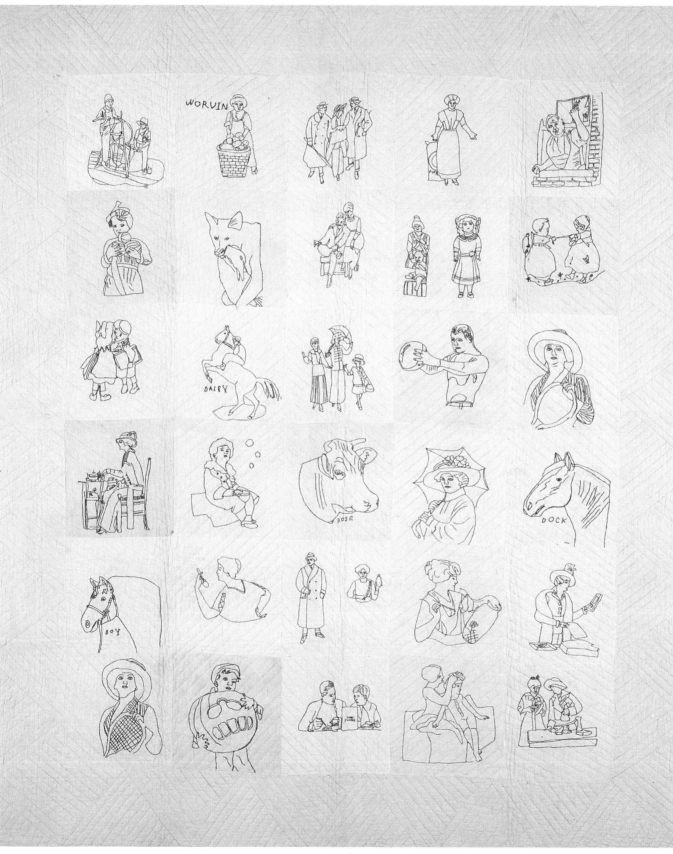

Norvin Marriner Quilt.

Norvin Marriner Quilt.

NORVIN MARRINER QUILT

Embroidered squares
Stark County, Ohio, 1917
Laura Fisher / antique quilts & Americana

The *Norvin Marriner Quilt* had a report card pinned to it when New York quilt dealer, historian and author Laura Fisher purchased it. The card was of Norvin Marriner, seventh grade, Talpahok School, Paris Township, Stark County, Ohio, with the date 1917. He was a good student—good to very good in everything but arithmetic and grammar—and on the basis of the card was promoted to eighth grade.

It is Ms. Fisher's assumption that this quilt was made for the boy and presented to him in recognition of his good report card—a presentation quilt, traditionally made to mark a rite of passage, like the freedom quilt made in colonial times to honor a man's twenty-first birthday.

The thirty scenes on the quilt are embroidered in red using an outline stitch on white squares. They appear to be predominantly scenes from the boy's and his family's life in Stark County, which in 1917 was and still is a rural area of Ohio. There are scenes of Norvin with a sack of potatoes, with a jack o' lantern, on a horse (Daisy), eating corn flakes with his father, watching a man making what appear to be barrel hoops, blowing bubbles; also, an irate man holding the ball that broke his window, and a man about to toss a basketball—all undoubtedly references to Norvin's favorite pastimes. There are other animals—two horses (Boy and Dock), and a cow (Rose). Other children are pictured, sisters, perhaps, and a baby on a chair, a girl holding an armful of melons, and a girl having her hairbow tied.

Although Norvin's family probably lived on a farm, there are signs of a more sophisticated life style in the quilt: elegantly dressed women shop-

141

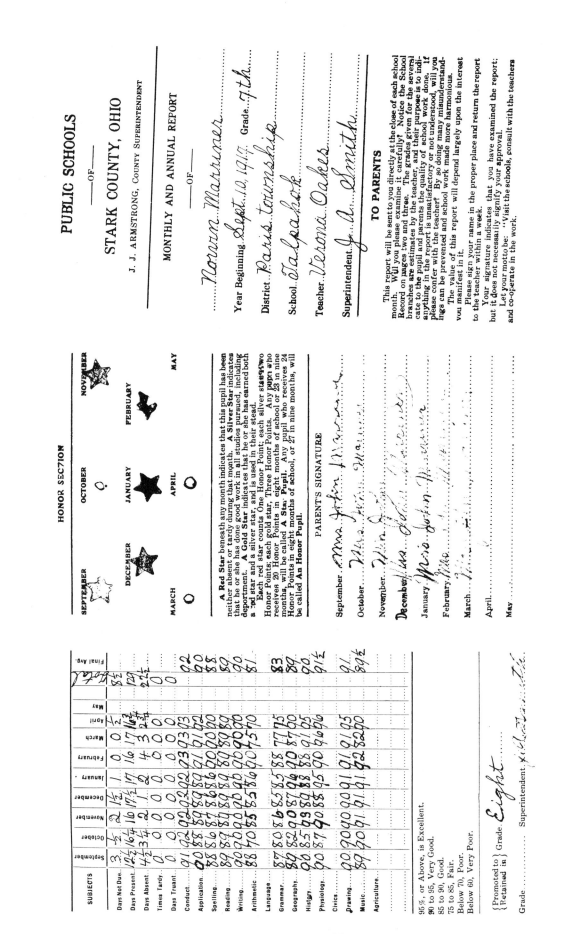

Norvin Marriner's seventh grade report card.

ping, painting a vase—china painting was popular at the time with women of leisure. It's possible that there was an aunt in nearby Canton, the county seat, from whom the more sophisticated elements of the quilt came. The mix of urban and country life is what makes this interesting as a historical document. There was no such thing as suburbia at the time, so that the distinctions between town and country were clearly defined.

It is possible that some of the pictures on the quilt were taken from purchased patterns—the babies playing tug o'war with a string, the girl kissing the little boy—these have a stilted look and lack the individuality of other scenes. The ladies with the tennis rackets—one has no strings—may be in this category too. It was common to buy patterns, which were taken from illustrations in story books for use in embroidery projects.

The quilting is done on diagonal lines, and the blocks assembled so that the quilting appears to be in a herringbone pattern. "Basket weave" more accurately describes the quilting in the outer border area.

Norvin Marriner Quilt.

Creation of the Animals Quilt.

Creation of the Animals Quilt.

PERSONAL VISIONS

The traditional quilt can only tell so much about the woman who made it. Hundreds of small pieces sewed into an intricate pattern suggest an avid quilter who enjoyed the challenge of putting pieces together, the more the better; or it could mean the quilter had limited means and had to salvage even the tiniest of scraps to acquire enough fabric to make a quilt top. Nor may choice of color be based only on the quilter's intention—grays and blacks to mourn a death, reds and greens to celebrate a marriage—but could well be related to financial status and ability to purchase fabrics imported from Europe or improved by the textile revolution that went hand in hand with the industrialization of America. Fanciful applique indicated a relative leisure; the more elaborate and fanciful the design, the more one assumes, the quilter's mind was free from domestic responsibilities to ponder and develop a unique design.

For most 19th century women, quilt making, whether for utilitarian or decorative purposes, was as expected and accepted an activity as cooking or knitting socks. Women quilted for their families and their pleasure; they quilted in competition with each other, as the women who made the album quilts in Baltimore did, and they showed off their quilts at fairs, the first arenas outside the home where women's domestic arts were displayed and judged. The huge array of quilts made in the 19th century tells a composite story of women, their cultural and domestic settings, social trends, and virtues, as well as productivity. The crazy quilt especially evidences a pastime. But except for occasional glimpses, the women themselves remain virtually invisible.

It is only in this century that quilts have begun to reveal the individual women's lives out of which they were created. Record keeping, communication, desire and determination to look behind the general for the particular, to study history and humans by studying individual lives—these trends have been adapted by thousands of women who are involved with quilts today. They are coupled with women's coming out of their houses and into the world, coming into their own, coming together to see increasingly that their lives are of value.

When quilts attracted a renewal of interest in the late '60s, it appeared to many to be just one more craft revival. However, its implications as a symbol of female and feminist qualities with links to the past had a great deal to do with its burgeoning popularity. The symbolic implications of the quilt, linked with the growing need for women to not only express themselves but define themselves, were important. (Currently quilting activities are an obsession among still-increasing numbers of women that has overflowed onto the shores of Great Britain, Australia, Japan and many other foreign countries). In classes and shops, at bees and exhibits, women have taken up the quilt as a form with few boundaries except the outside measurements which the quilter herself is free to choose. The quilt, as it is made today, has meaning as a symbol for women's increased opportunities. Interest in quilts implies a growing curiosity and interest in what women stand for, and have stood for, in our culture. The quilt has made a very long journey from its use in mourning family deaths (*The Graveyard Quilt*) to something as personal, celebratory, rule-breaking—and mundane—as Faith Ringgold's confessional quilt celebrating her triumph in her lifelong battle with food and excess pounds.

Besides the long journey from bedcover to personal statement, the quilt has undertaken another long journey, one that has been described as a leap: from bed to gallery wall. It was the art establishment's attentions to the quilt that started quilters—men as well as women—on this journey. In the '60s op art and minimalist movements in painting inspired two important art exhibitions. One, at the Newark Art Museum in 1965, displayed quilts focusing on aesthetic merits rather than craftsmanship. The other, Abstract Design in American Quilts, was held at the Whitney Museum in New York in 1971. Since then, the art world has been gradually accepting the quilt form as one worthy of being displayed along with painting and sculpture. Women have experimented, achieved and sometimes triumphed with the art quilt. In 1978, in response to a growing trend among quilt artists, the first Quilt National exhibit was held in Athens, Ohio, as an arena for display of this new art form. The purpose was to "carry definition of quilting far beyond its traditional parameters and to promote quilt making as what it always has been—an art form."* The first show drew 190 submitters who entered 390 works; the 1989 exhibit attracted 1154 entries by 560 artists from 44 states and twelve foreign countries.

Although innovation is a hallmark of the art quilt, clearly the influence of the early quilt makers is palpable in most of these works. The influence of the past, the desire to work with textiles, the desire to make a personal statement and the desire to participate in a tradition with links to the past are pieced together in the same spirit in which colonial women pieced together their quilts—but with freedom and opportunity replacing harsh necessity.

Personal Visions is not a sampling of popular and ordinary styles whose designs are accessible to all quilters and easy to reproduce. The four artists—for their work is considered art—represented here are out of the ordinary and unique, for several reasons. Their work reflects a personal and creative vision each has been able to realize, given the constraints of individual limitations, opportunities, and cultural settings. One is a folk artist whose quilts typify the art form "that represents the unconventional in American art . . . created by persons of little or no training whose good hands and sharp eyes . . . incorporated in their creativeness the attitudes of a people and a reflection of their social history."** The other three women are artists in a post-feminist world where they have combined quilting and fine arts traditions, then broken those traditions in order to define themselves. For them there are no limits.

Quilt National, General Information Sheet.

**p. 155, *Nineteenth-Century Folk Painting: Our Spirited National Heritage*. The William Benton Museum of Art, 1973.

THE CREATION OF THE ANIMALS

Appliqued cotton with embroidery
By Harriet Powers
Georgia, c. 1886
The Museum of Fine Arts
Bequest of Maxim Karolik
105 inches by 69 inches

Creation of the Animals has a balance of Bible tales, astronomical events and folk lore. Further, it suggests that Mrs. Powers had in mind a parallel between her own fate and that of the biblical figures from the Old Testament she chose to represent: Moses, Noah, Jonah and Job all experienced God's harsh judgment but also his power to deliver them from frightening circumstances. Each man's agony foreshadows the salvation offered by Christ as well as Mrs. Powers' deliverance from slavery.

Of equal importance in the second quilt are events in the skies, which Mrs. Powers would have heard about locally and which scholars confirm

> The sun did disappear on May 19, 1780. The seven stars and trumpet were New Testament symbols for Judgment Day. History confirms that many New Englanders feared the end of the world had come (square 2)

> On November 13, 1833, there was in fact an eight-hour meteor shower (square 8)

> Thursday, February 10, 1895, was indeed a day of record-breaking cold (square 11)

> Bells were rung on a night in 1846 to tell people of the mysterious red light (square 12)

A third influence in the *Creation of the Animals* is legend, most specifically in square 13, where the figure of the hog Bett is portrayed. According to local folk narrative, Bett walked 500 miles from Georgia to Virginia. Bett is the most prominent figure in the quilt, placed in a conspicuous position. Her flight followed the same route runaway slaves took before the Civil War. While Mrs. Powers did not have the artistic permission or language to tell the story of slavery's end in more subjective terms, she has woven it in with the other elements of her quilt.

The care Mrs. Powers took making the sun, moon and stars, which are pieced and appliqued, as opposed to the figures of humans and animals, each of which is cut from one piece of cloth and machine-sewn to the quilt, suggests that weather occurences inspired her with fear and awe. Perhaps

this was because news of these events was passed on by real people who had witnessed them.

A visionary who accepted her fate—of her slavery years she only expressed nostalgia for her "ole miss"—Mrs. Powers reveals nothing of the hardships of slavery except by implication in the tribulations of the biblical heroes who, like the slaves, were eventually freed and redeemed. The quilt does not tell her personal history but she was able to record in woman's creative form stories of threat, deliverance and freedom, brought down to earth, or to human scale. It is typical of her up-bringing as inferior in status to white folk that the figures she depicts were all white.

There is much speculation that Mrs. Powers' style is rooted in the appliqued tapestries of Dahomey, in West Africa. If this is the case, she might have learned techniques from older slaves in the house where she served. The possibility that her quilts have roots in Africa make them stories of a long journey—from Africa into slavery and out into freedom.

Harriet Powers.

Sacred Heart Garden Quilt.

Sacred Heart Garden Quilt.

SACRED HEART GARDEN

Applique and embroidery, painted fabric, and embellishments
By Terrie Hancock Mangat, 1988
Bernice Steinbaum Gallery
96 inches by 91 inches

Sacred Heart Garden quilt takes a backward look at Terrie Hancock Mangat's life, even as it travels inward to explore the artist's psychic landscape. Shaped like a head, it is a self-analysis of a woman who has reflected on what is important for her to protect from society's traditional threats to woman's selfhood. The artist explains that it is about "keeping the stones intact around one's interior. If one or two stones are taken away, it leaves a hole in the wall and the weed of depression comes in and strangles the precious plants." (The purple weed in the lower left corner is labeled as such, and forces its way into the interior of the garden through a break. The tentacles have a stranglehold on the daisy, a painted fabric detail.)

Further explaining the work, Terrie Mangat goes

on, "In this garden, the plants represent what is sacred to me and what is important to my wellbeing." Each of these features of her life grows out of a heart (Look carefully at the base of the trees for the hearts; many are difficult to recognize because they are appliqued from printed fabric and they tend to blend with the background). "Time to do what I feel is important" is a plant that grows wristwatches; "my children" is portrayed in cut-out figures on a plant with deep green stems. "Parental relations" are represented by portraits of Terrie and of her parents which spring from a shimmery blue tree growing from a red and blue heart. Gold-colored fabric figures in various floor exercise positions are the fruit of a pink shrub springing from a green and pink plaid heart below left center to

Sacred Heart Garden Quilt.

indicate the importance of "exercise." Other plants growing from hearts produce "spirituality," "good food," "friendship," "art," "freedom to be me," and "marriage."

Mangat's garden is protected by variously quilted and colored stones; the color brown is added for the dirt necessary to grow the plants. Follow this colored stone border around the garden, noticing sequins individually applied between the stones. As you examine the left border of the garden, find the roots of the Weed of Depression—they are identified as guilt, jealousy, and greed—which must be guarded against at all costs.

As you examine the upper portions of the stone border, look at the adjacent representations for the grass. Pieces of zippers of different colors denote some of the blades of grass—the shimmer is the metal zipper teeth. Green metallic paint gives additional glow to this area. In the top center of the quilt in the blue sky, silver baguettes fall from the heavens. Just below this area and slightly to the right is a yellow-branched tree that grows ballet shoes, soccer balls, diving figures, a baseball player, a hockey player, sailboats, tennis racket, snorkler, and skate board—all of the things that control the lives of many mothers these days. The spirituality tree is below that with the figures of saints, and in toward the center is a tree with artist's brushes and palettes. Moving down into the lower corner, the

crinkling in the grass area is caused by lines of stitching that do not run parallel. Blue sequins edge the plaid grass which is quilted in squares. Terrie has signed the quilt in pink script in this corner, just above the blue edging that glitters with silver dots.

Using the quilt, which has become a contemporary symbol for womanhood, Mangat has created a personal statement—first as an artist, breaking down barriers of materials, techniques and subject matter, but also as a woman. What is really sacred to this artist is her selfhood.

*Shrine to the
Beginning Quilt.*

SHRINE TO THE BEGINNING

Applique and embroidery with other embellishments
By Terrie Hancock Mangat, 1987
Bernice Steinbaum Gallery

Shrine to the Beginning started as a map of the farm where Terrie Mangat lived with her husband in her early marriage and where she took her first steps toward independence, but she put it aside when she felt herself and her life changing.

Mangat has always been aware of the controversy over whether her works are quilts or art; in fact, in her work as in that of other quilt-artists, the lines between the two disciplines are blurred. "Alot of quilters think that my quilts have too much 'junk' and weirdness to be quilts," she says, "but non-art-educated people feel something strongly about them. The fabric helps everyday people to relate to the piece. Maybe quilts are the 'working-man's art.' I feel like my quilts are on the outer edge of being quilts (some of them) and some are on the outer edge of art. They are straddling the line like alot of other things in my life."*

*p. 222, *America's Glorious Quilts*.

In 1987, ten years after she began exhibiting her work, Mangat went back to *Shrine to the Beginning*. She realized she could finish the quilt in the style she was then working in. "I made the old quilted farm the object of the shrine," she says, "painted new parts, recycled parts of defunct projects." From her saints work evolved the two saints standing in the foreground; Terrie as St. Theresa, her patron saint, and her husband as the Little Flower, St. Francis. (She's quick to deny any claims to saint-hood. "We're just occupants of that particular shrine.") The jewel-like colors are achieved with silks, cottons and painted canvas. To embroidery and quilting, she's added milagros (religious medals hung by Mexicans on statutes to reinforce a prayer, like lighting a candle), painted charms, pre-packaged appliques, buttons and beads. "The result is a summation of my experiences to that point in my life," she says of *Shrine to the Beginning*: It's her "homage to my growth as an individual."

Heart Attack Quilt.

Heart Attack Quilt.

HEART ATTACK

Applique and reverse applique in vinyl and assorted fabrics
By Deborah J. Felix
California, 1987
Collection of the Artist
70 inches by 91 inche'

Heart Attack, even though it has only one figure, is about a relationship. One that was breaking up when she created the composition, says artist Deborah Felix. "My work is about me, narcissistic, self-indulgent. I was going through a divorce, feeling my heart thumping so hard I was having anxiety attacks. It's also about how when something terrible is happening to us we think it's the worst thing in the world. But it isn't. We live through it."

"I came to quilting strictly out of necessity," says Felix. Although her Fine Arts degree was in textiles, she didn't attempt quilting until she tried to simplify the molas she was making into more manageable wallpieces. (Molas are fabric creations originally done by natives of Central America using a technique like reverse applique, but with several layers of fabric.) Quilting allowed her to move from five or six layers of fabric to two layers. "I started with machine quilting pieces, then hand quilted a

piece when I was asked to submit to an exhibit and a book.* The label 'quilter' was sort of placed on me, since my work filled the definition."

Felix feels use of fabric in her work keeps her out of fine arts galleries, though she senses that this attitude is changing. She definitely does not consider herself a quilter. "I have quilted," she says, "and very poorly at that." Presently she has someone else quilt her pieces. "I use quilting as a structural element and not a design element. . . . When I teach quilting techniques I teach about how to go about creating the concepts that are in one's head, and without a pattern. I try to teach people how to look at their work as an art form. I think my true love is teaching about art as a whole." Her approach to her own work she describes as "painterly." She works with fabric pinned to the wall, and cuts away layers as for reverse applique. She sews and paints standing up.

153

Her larger-than-life wall pieces are self portraits done with distance and humor, and a dash of post-modern neurosis. She describes the spirit of her works as looking at life's traumas with the attitude that "one must laugh at . . . failures and successes in life and keep plodding on with blind faith in the future." Her earlier pieces concentrate on couples engaged in their daily activities, and have offbeat, humorous titles: *Fred Wants at Least a Cracker, Discussing Plants for the Future, She Loved Words So Much They Lost Their Meaning.* Each one showed a specific environment—a kitchen, a living room—decorated with patterned fabrics done in warm intimate colors. Although the backgrounds she created could be anyone's home, anywhere, Felix usually included a teapot (she collects them). Against the detailed background, the figure were abstracted.

In *Heart Attack,* the figure doesn't have a physical problem, she has an emotional one. Notice the heart on her arm (sleeve). Felix copied the pose

from a picture she ripped from a medical magazine in which a person was having a gallstone attack. The setting is her own living room, reproduced in painted and fabric prints. The wallpaper pattern is reminiscent of quilt block-and-border patterns. The patterned vinyl recalls the kitchen linoleum of her childhood.

The quilting of *Heart Attack* is done in the ditch (on the very seam line), as a structural, not a design, element. But it does add depth to the design. The shadings of the flesh tones and the hair are obviously done with paint—hair detailing has been added with an object used as a stamp. The still life on the yellow table is also painted—note the signature in the right corner of the table. Green leaves and tendrils on the pink sofa cushions are added over printed fabric, and the wall tiles and windows have additions in paint. Note also that some of the outer layers are transparent, giving a feeling of dimension to the quilt.

The Art Quilt. Penny McMorris and Michael Kile, The Quilt Digest Press, 198 .

I LOST MY WEDDING RING IN THE DESERT

Mix of applique and reverse applique in vinyl and assorted fabrics
By Deborah J. Felix
California, 1988
Collection of the Artist

I Lost My Wedding Ring in the Desert was completed by Deborah Felix after a move from the East coast to California. The move marked a decided shift in subject matter and use of fabric in her quilts. Earlier work was much influenced by her having spent much of her life in Western New York State, an area not noted for a beneficent or bright climate. Her recent works are set outdoors under a much stronger West coast light. "When I first moved to California," says the artist, "I was so amazed by the desert, I cut my hair, and had someone take my picture."

I Lost My Wedding Ring recognizes a chapter in her personal history, the symbolic putting behind of the wrecked marriage that inspired *Heart Attack.* It is Felix's second outdoor piece, done after her California move. It shines with a vinyl Pacific and bright green cactus plants. Staring out at the

viewer is the artist, wearing trendy dark glasses. The background, made up of patterned and painted fabric, also has stamped embellishments on the rocks and sand. The in-the-ditch stitching adds contours to the objects, and the transparency of the outer layer of fabric in some places adds depth. Subjective though it is, the figure confronts the viewer in a bold way that draws the viewer into her artistic and personal vision. Although there is only one figure, the work is still about relation-ships—the individual as a single person in her relationship with herself. Felix has traveled far to a confrontation with innermost thoughts about love, death and the future. She has also traveled far from the traditional quilt and its materials and techniques to challenge the art world and its resistance to valuing work like hers as fine art.

I Lost My Wedding Ring in the Desert Quilt.

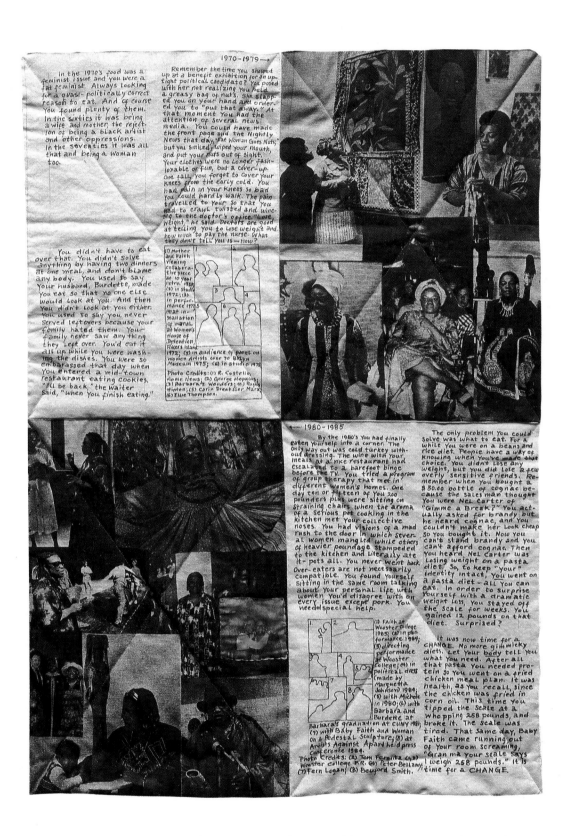

CHANGE: Faith Ringgold's Over 100 Pounds Weight Loss Quilt.

C. LOVE

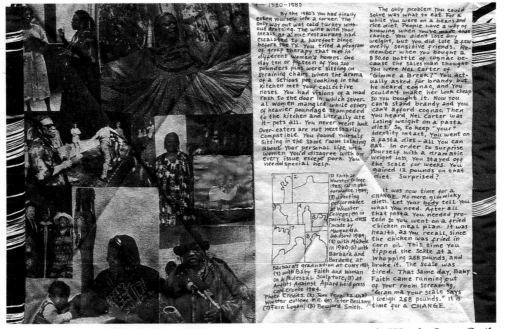

CHANGE: Faith Ringgold's Over 100 Pounds Weight Loss Quilt.

CHANGE: Faith Ringgold's Over 100 Pounds Weight Loss Quilt

By Faith Ringgold
1986
Bernice Steinbaum Gallery

CHANGE: Faith Ringgold's Over 100 Pounds Weight Loss Story Quilt has a narrative hand-printed on fabric with indelible markers. Growing up in Harlem, Faith Ringgold learned two cultural and family traditions from her mother: sewing and storytelling. A major figure in the feminist and Black art movements of the 1960s, Ringgold has used her richly narrative story quilts to speak out on Afro-American history, civil rights, her own childhood and her struggles as a Black woman and artist, wife, mother and political activist.

Even before she arrived at her story quilt form of expression, Ringgold incorporated a strong narrative sense into her work. In the '60s her mural-size paintings made strong visual statements about racial conflict and discrimination. In the '70s her

157

works began to move off the canvas, expanding into the use of masks and soft sculptures and confronting the issues of Black aesthetics and the realities of Black women's lives. By the late '70s her works were weaving back and forth between Black history and personal history, African beliefs and American folk tales. In 1979 she was asked to create a quilt for a show by women artists. The work, *Echoes of Harlem,* was her last collaboration with her mother, dressmaker and fashion designer Willi Posey, who had sewn the fabric frames and clothes for soft sculptures in Ringgold's earlier works. *Echoes of Harlem* changed Ringgold's development as an artist. It enabled her to realize that the quilt, so intimately connected with women's lives, could become an effective form for telling the stories of their lives.

Having taken up the causes of her race and her sex, and celebrated women, Black women in particular, Ringgold, in the late '80s was ready finally to celebrate herself. The form she chose for her CHANGE quilt was a strong individual statement which separated her from the "collective anonymous" quilt makers who had gone before her. In her autobiographical quilt she took up the weight problem that had plagued her since childhood, a problem she felt she had used to hide behind while achieving success. In it, fifteen blocks alternate text and photoetched collage, pieced fabric and fragmented narrative, to tell the story of a woman transformed from "what she is expected to be into

Faith Ringgold.

what she wants to be." The X-quilting on the text is appropriate for a celebration of changing, of eradicating the past.

Faith Ringgold does a performance to accompany the exhibition of this quilt. Wearing a jacket identical to the quilt, she drags the equivalent of the 100 pounds in plastic bottles full of water on stage, raps, dances and sings to the accompaniment of African percussion rhythms.

SOUTH AFRICAN LOVE STORY, Parts 1 and 2

Intaglio on canvas; painted and pieced fabric
By Faith Ringgold
1985-87
Bernice Steinbaum Gallery
64 inches by 79 inches

In *South African Love Story, Parts 1 and 2*, the text is printed horizontally like newspaper headlines against vertical and horizontal strips of bright fabric. It tells the story of Sheba, whose mother, daughter of a MaiMai chief, works as a maid in Soweto and whose father carves funeral statues for white people. "Making angels out of sinners," Sheba says, and "getting those devils into heaven instead of hell." Sheba and her lover Batu vow

to live their lives together in the struggle to be free, to end the pass laws, and abolish apartheid. Batu is imprisoned; Sheba escapes to London, where she becomes a model. She hears that her mother has been shot in the demolition of their village for racial rezoning. In the second quilt, Sheba is in New York City. She is reunited with Batu at a Madison Avenue gallery which is exhibiting masks from West Africa. In the end they

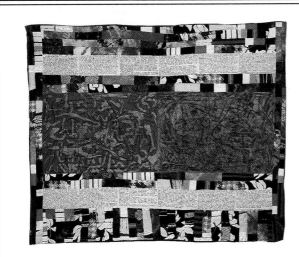

South African Love Story Quilt.

return to South Africa to get his mother out of jail, and resume the struggle for freedom.

The centers of these quilts are done in intaglio, fabric printed from etched zinc plates which are superimposed on top of each other. Ringgold likes the spontaneity of etching, calling it exciting: "You never know what it's going to look like when it's printed." She says these quilts have a strong feeling of South Africa for her—jumpy, crazy. The shapes in the center intaglio area echo writhing ghostly human shapes. The shapes represent not only South African Blacks but all Blacks enslaved over centuries. She is speaking out against all enslavement, including sexual enslavement by white men.

Ringgold says the shapes in the center area are also about the individual's trying to get space for herself, establish an individual identity, find a room for her own. She is portraying the struggle against societal compacting into tiny spaces and categories such as "black," "woman," and "woman artist," when what a woman seeks is acceptance as an individual for her own individual work.

CHURCH PICNIC PAINTED QUILT

Painted canvas; pieced, dyed and painted fabric
By Faith Ringgold
1988
High Museum, Atlanta
76 inches square

Church Picnic Painted Quilt is a creation that brings together old themes and stories assembled with many elements from traditional quilting to represent Black culture, its roots, and where it stands now. An offbeat framework of triangles surrounds what appears to be an idealized portrait of a Baptist church picnic. But the text and many of the details suggest something else. Racism lurks behind the word "Freedom" on the sign: white people have chased the picnickers away from their former gathering place because they didn't want colored there. "Someday we gonna be free." says the narrator to her daughter, Aleathia; but, the artist reminds us, "We are not free yet."

Another theme of the quilt is betrayal, and the inconstancy of men. "These men folk is a mess," says the narrator, whose daughter has been forgotten by the reverend, whom she loves, now ena-moured of a woman just back from missionary work in Africa. Eyes flash and dart from faces, lending a jumpiness to the scene, linking the picnickers to the dangers of life and love and death. (Ringgold recalls being at dinner as a child, and watching adults' eyes flash signals to each other to make certain the kids were protected from knowing the worst of what they were discussing.) At the picnic there is even an ominous quality to the play of the boys and girls in the foreground, males in pursuit, females at risk.

And yet, of course, this is a joyful and colorful scene. Calico and striped fabrics, the Baptist church, missionary work, the plentitude of food the women have prepared, the churchgoers dressed in Sunday best—Ringgold has used paintbrush and needle to portray the dazzling vitality of Black culture.

Bibliography

Baker, Barbara, ed. *The State of the Art Quilt: Contemporary Quilts for the Collector.* Published in conjunction with Quilt Expo '85 exhibition at Sands Point, New York.

Bank, Mirra. *Anonymous Was a Woman.* St. Martin's Press, 1979.

Bishop, Robert. *New Discoveries in American Quilts.* E.P. Dutton, 1975.

Bishop, Robert and Carleton L. Stafford. *America's Quilts and Coverlets.* Weathervane Books, 1974.

Cooper, Patricia, and Norma Bradley Buferd. *The Quilters: Women and Domestic Art.* AnchorPress/Doubleday, 1978.

Duke, Dennis and Deborah Harding, ed. *America's Glorious Quilts.* Dis by MacMillan Publishing Co., Hugh Lauter Levin Associates, Inc., 1987.

Edwards, Ann and Deidre Windsor, res. "The Virginia Ivey Quilts: Nineteenth Century Masterworks." *Needlearts,* XVIII, Vol. 3, August 1987.

Ferrero, Pat, Elaine Hedges, and Julie Silber. *Hearts and Hands: The Influence of Women and Quilts on American Society.* The Quilt Digest Press, 1987.

Ferris, William. *Afro-American Folk Art and Crafts.* University Press of Mississippi, 1983.

Ferris, William. *Local Color: A Sense of Place in Folk Art.* McGraw-Hill Book Company, 1982.

Gouma-Peterson. "Faith Ringgold's Narrative Quilts," *Faith Ringgold Change: Painted Story Quilts.* Bernice Steinbaum Gallery.

Gutcheon, Beth. *The Perfect Patchwork Primer.* David McKay Company, Inc., 1973.

Hancock, Lyn Nell and Paula Nadelstern. *Quilting Together.* Crown Publishers, 1988.

Ickis, Margeurite. *The Standard Book of Quilt Making and Collecting.* Dover Publications, Inc., New York, 1949.

James, Michael. *The Quiltmaker's Handbook.* Prentice-Hall, 1978.

Katzenberg, Dena S. *Baltimore Album Quilts.* The Baltimore Museum of Art, 1981.

Kentucky Quilt Project, *Kentucky Quilts 1800-1900.* Pantheon, 1982.

Leon, Eli. "Who'd A Thought It?" Catalog, San Francisco Craft and Folk Art Museum, 1987.

Lipsett, Linda Otto. *Remember Me: Women and Their Friendship Quilts.* The Quilt Digest Press, 1985.

Macdonald, Anne L. *No Idle Hands: The Social History of American Knitting.* Ballantine Books, 1988.

Nineteenth-Century Folk Painting: Our Spirited National Heritage. The William Benton Museum of Art, 1973.

Orlofsky, Patsy and Myron. *Quilts in America.* McGraw-Hill Book Company, 1974.

Oshins, Lisa Turner. *Quilt Collections: A Directory for the United States and Canada.*

Roth, Moira. "The Field and the Drawing Room," *Faith Ringgold Change: Painted Story Quilts.* Bernice Steinbaum Gallery.

Texas Heritage Society. *Texas Quilts, Texas Treasures.* American Quilter's Society, Paduceh, KY, 1986.

Wahlman, Maude Southwell. "African-American Quilts: Tracing the Aesthetic Principles," *The Clarion: America's Folk Art Magazine.* Spring, 1989, Vol. 14, No. 2.